To Andrew

CONTENTS

INTRODUCTION

I fell in love with cooking when I moved to California after design school in 2009. When I first arrived in Berkeley, I got a job at a French restaurant while I was trying to figure out how to navigate postcollege life. The restaurant was small and had an open kitchen, which gave me the amazing opportunity to observe the pros in action. There, I was introduced to seasonal cooking and making things from scratch: Nothing came from packages, all the ingredients were local, and everything — right down to the condiments — was made in house. It was a new way of thinking about food, and I found it very exciting. It was around this time that I started drawing all the food I was cooking at home. I wanted to share all the techniques I was learning, and I needed the artistic outlet, so in 2010 I started my blog, Illustrated Bites. After that, everything began to fall into place.

There is a definite food mantra here in the San Francisco Bay Area — eat fresh and eat local — and I've totally bought in. And the freshest and most local produce you can get is that which you've grown yourself. Growing your own vegetables and small fruits connects you with what is in season. After you get accustomed to growing cycles, you'll start raising your eyebrows at certain things, like when you see blueberries at the store in December. The recipes I developed for this book are "produce-centric," they reflect what's seasonally available, and they're made from whole and minimally processed ingredients. The recipes don't require any special equipment, and they're not complicated or fussy. The best food is really simple.

These days we're all busy, and a good way to recenter and slow down is to focus on mealtime. It's important to nourish our bodies and share good food and conversation with those who are dear to us. When I have a busy week of being buried in endless tasks, when I feel like every free second is spent checking my phone, the anxiety and stress starts wearing on me in a deep way. Getting my hands dirty in the kitchen or the garden has a way of melting that stress away. Come harvest time, when I cook the vegetables I've grown myself, I feel such gratitude for my food because I know the time and effort it took to get it to my plate. I would love to have a lifestyle in which I could spend every day in the garden and every evening cooking delicious meals. But the truth is that a girl's got to pay her rent. However, the weekend mornings when I tend my garden and the weekdays when I water my greens and maybe pull a few weeds are precious and calming respites from the hectic modern world. I won't argue that we should all give up going to the grocery store and strive to be completely self-sufficient, but I do know that gardening and home cooking foster a mindfulness and calm that we all could use.

Just start with a small container garden, cook a few seasonal dishes, and see where it takes you.

THE UNPROCESSED PANTRY

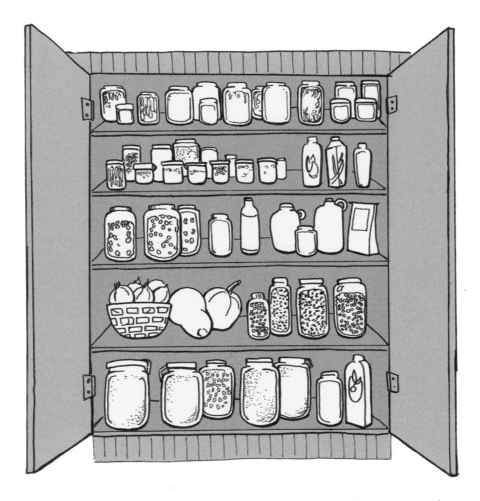

Eating unprocessed foods is a way to get more whole, natural goodness into your diet. The idea behind eating unprocessed is to avoid eating too much of anything that is refined and prepackaged. If you keep your pantry well stocked, it will make all of your kitchen projects—from throwing together a quick weekday meal to baking quick breads—go much more smoothly. It's a matter of changing how you think about ingredients and their potential. When building your own unprocessed pantry, you should start with some whole ingredients, spices, and dry goods that you can keep at the ready to help you prepare simple, nutritious meals.

PANTRY STAPLES

KITCHEN BASICS

ESSENTIAL TOOLS FOR EVERYDAY COOKING

While you certainly don't need every gadget out there, tools like vegetable peelers can make life easier when starting out in the kitchen. I'm usually of the opinion that tools should have more than one function, but sometimes you just have to wonder *what have I been doing?* when you switch from a paring knife to a swivel peeler, or two forks to a whisk. Here are a few tools I find handy when diving into the recipes in this book.

BAKING DISHES

SKILLETS

BAKING SHEET

MEASURING CUPS & SPOONS

CUTTING BOARDS

WHISK

FOOD PROCESSOR

WOODEN SPOONS

IMMERSION BLENDER

KNIVES

ROLLING PIN

METAL COLANDER

ELECTRIC MIXER

SAUCEPAN

LARGE POT

SMALL KITCHEN SCALE

STOCKPOT

VEGETABLE PEELER

GARDENING BASICS

ESSENTIAL TOOLS FOR GARDENING

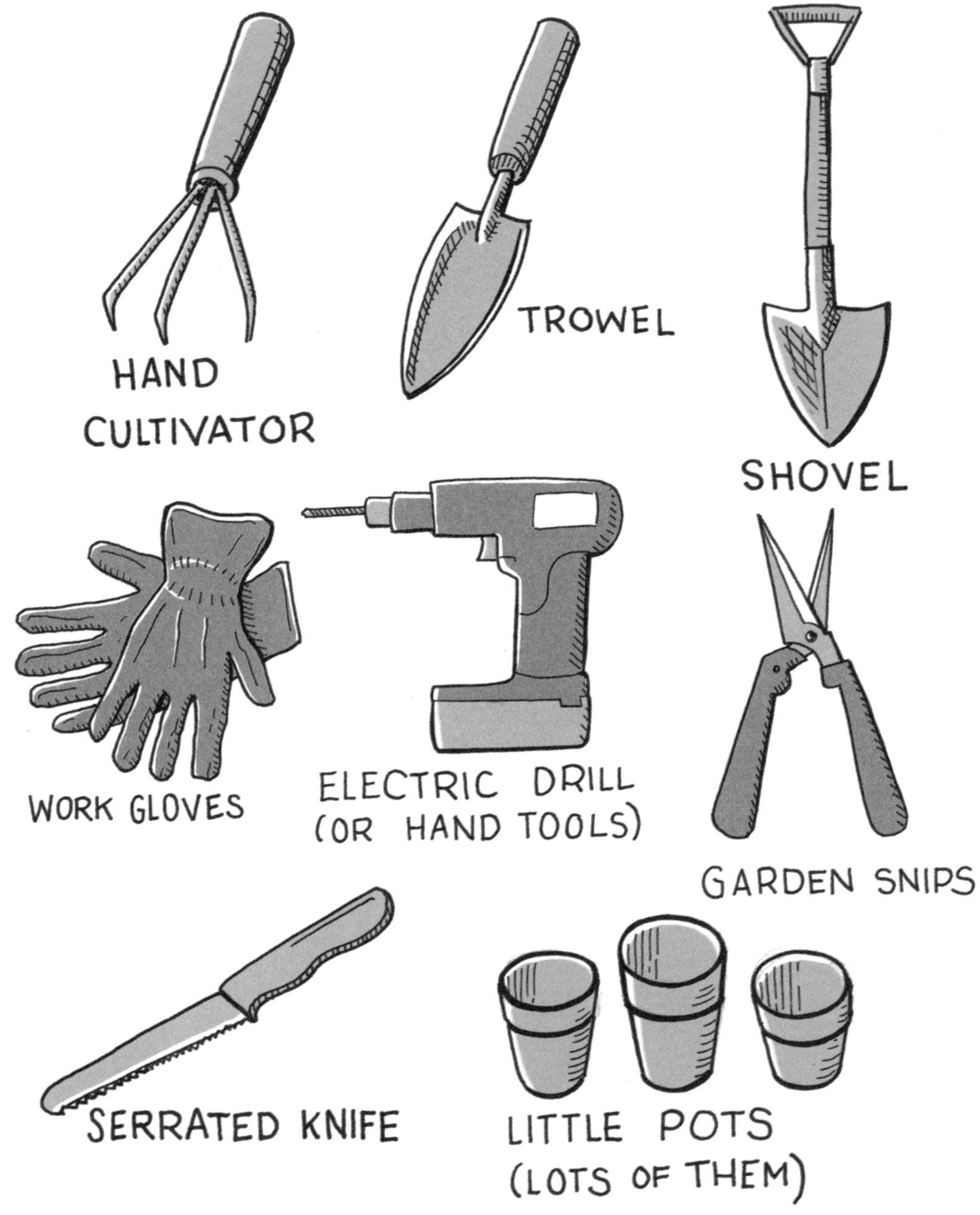

HAND CULTIVATOR

TROWEL

SHOVEL

WORK GLOVES

ELECTRIC DRILL
(OR HAND TOOLS)

GARDEN SNIPS

SERRATED KNIFE

LITTLE POTS
(LOTS OF THEM)

GARDENING ANYWHERE

If you're interested in gardening but aren't lucky enough to have a yard, you shouldn't let that stop you. Sunny patios, front steps, or even building rooftops are great places for container gardens. Even if you only have a sunny window, you can still have a few homegrown veggies indoors. In urban areas, taking part in community gardens is also a great way to access green space and hang out with like-minded folks.

CONTAINER GARDENING

You can use any large container for your crops, as long as it's waterproof and has drainage. Five-gallon (19-L) buckets, found wine crates, old dresser drawers, and giant olive oil tins are all possibilities as long as you drill drainage holes into the bottom. If you plan to use unfinished wooden containers, treat them with Danish or linseed oil first to seal them and keep them from rotting. Garden soil is too dense for containers; it doesn't let enough air around the roots or hold the right amount of moisture. Use organic potting soil for smaller containers. For larger containers, stretch the potting soil by mixing 4 parts potting soil, 1 part sand, 2 parts compost, and 1 cup organic fertilizer per cubic foot.

RAISED BEDS

Build your raised bed out of wood that hasn't been chemically treated; cedar is a good choice, as it's naturally rot resistant. Seal it with linseed or Danish oil. You can also use bricks or cinderblocks to frame your bed. Double dig the soil by digging through the topsoil and loosening the subsoil. Mix in plenty of compost, manure, and shredded leaves. If your garden soil is very rocky or mostly clay, just fill the whole bed with manure or compost. Build the bed in the fall and let the manure mellow over the winter for planting in the spring.

BASIC RAISED BED

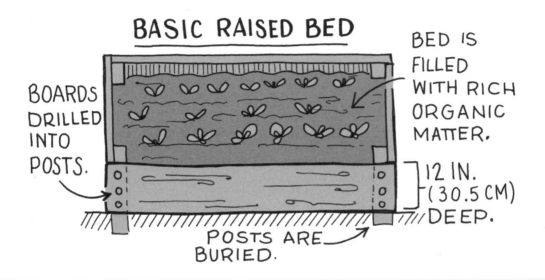

BED IS FILLED WITH RICH ORGANIC MATTER.

BOARDS DRILLED INTO POSTS.

12 IN. (30.5 CM) DEEP.

POSTS ARE BURIED.

ANNUALS VS. BIENNIALS VS. PERENNIALS

Annuals are plants that complete their entire life cycle in one growing season. They germinate, flower, produce seeds, and die within one year, so they have to be replanted every year. Biennials are plants that require two growing seasons to complete their life cycle. They grow the first year and flower and go to seed the second year. Perennials live for many growing seasons. They may die back in the winter, but the roots survive and regrow the plant the following year.

GROW & DIE

FLOWER, THEN DIE

CONTINUOUS CYCLES OF GROWTH

YEAR 1 (ANNUALS)

YEAR 2 (BIENNIALS)

YEAR 3 + (PERENNIALS)

ORGANIC GARDENING

Simply put, organic gardening is the process of growing fruits and vegetables without synthetic fertilizers and pesticides. Building up the soil by adding compost (see page 16), planting legumes, and rotating your crops are organic ways of providing nutrients for your plants. Organic gardening is better for wildlife and beneficial insects, like ladybugs and bees. It also reduces your own contact with synthetic chemicals, since you won't be using those herbicides, pesticides, and petrochemicals on your dinner.

USE COMPOST & MANURE

OR

LIQUID KELP

NOT

FAKE
SYNTHETIC PETRO-CHEMICAL FERTILIZER

• USE FLOATING ROW COVERS.
• HANDPICK SLUGS & SNAILS.
• BLAST APHIDS OFF WITH WATER.
• PULL WEAK PLANTS.
• REMOVE DEAD FOLIAGE.

INSECT KILLING SOAP

OKAY

DON'T USE

BUG-X
KILLS ALL!

NO-KAY

MULCH TO SUPPRESS WEEDS

AND

REMOVE WEEDS BY HAND

DON'T USE

WEED KILLER

SOIL QUALITY AND COMPOSTING

Healthy soil is alive and full of microorganisms, insects, and worms. The main mac-ronutrients in soil that plants need for growth are nitrogen, phosphorus, and potas-sium. There are also many secondary micronutrients that contribute to the health of the plant. As plants grow, they consume these nutrients, and over time the soil can be depleted. Keeping these nutrients in balance maintains soil health. Rotating what you plant in your garden with legumes (such as peas) is a method for keeping the soil healthy. Legumes have nitrogen-fixing bacteria on their roots that take nitrogen out of the air and return it to the soil.

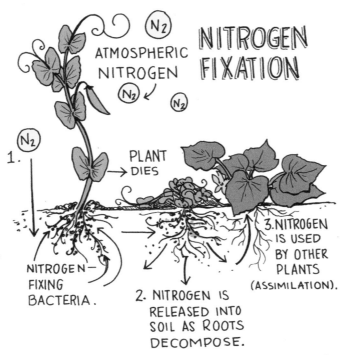

Another way to keep your soil healthy is by composting. Composting is the natural process in which worms and microorganisms break down organic matter into rich soil. A compost pile outside is a great way to turn yard clippings, fallen leaves, and kitchen scraps into nutritious soil for your garden. Start your own pile by mixing together 3 parts brown ingredients (high-carbon organic matter) to 1 part green ingredients

3 PARTS BROWN

DRIED LEAVES

UNTREATED SAWDUST

DRIED GARDEN DEBRIS

1 PART GREEN

GRASS CLIPPINGS

KITCHEN SCRAPS

ANIMAL MANURE

(high-nitrogen organic matter), with a few shovelfuls of soil. Every few weeks, use a pitchfork to turn your compost. When it is black and crumbly, it's ready to be used in the garden. If the pile is well managed it will break down in about three months.

VERMICOMPOSTING

Vermicomposting uses red wriggler worms in a bin to eat your extra kitchen scraps and turn them into nutrient-rich worm castings (worm poop). One pound (455 g) of red wrigglers can consume about 3½ pounds (1.6 kg) of kitchen scraps in a week. Vermicomposting is a good option for small spaces: Worm bins can be kept under the sink, in the garage, or on the porch.

RICH COMPOST COMES OUT.

KITCHEN SCRAPS GO IN.

STARTING FROM SEEDS

Starting plants from seed gives you the opportunity to order a wider variety of culitvars and select only the strongest plants for your garden; it is much cheaper than buying young plants. Depending on what you're planting and the length of your growing season, you can either sow the seeds directly into the ground or start the seedlings indoors to give them a head start.

HOW TO START SEEDS INDOORS

1. TO START SEEDS INDOORS, FIRST CUT A HOLE IN A SMALL PLASTIC CUP FOR DRAINAGE.

2. FILL 3/4 FULL WITH SEED-STARTING MIX OR POTTING SOIL & WET THOROUGLY WITH A SPRAY BOTTLE.

3. POKE A HOLE AT THE DEPTH RECOMMENDED ON THE SEED PACKET.

4. DROP A SEED IN THE HOLE & SPRINKLE SOIL OVER THE SEED.

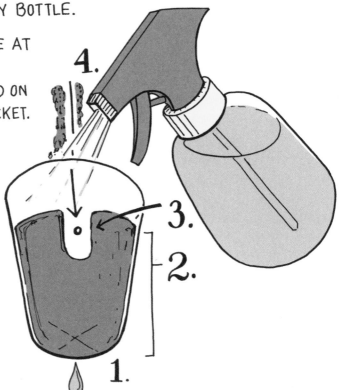

All seedlings need plenty of light to thrive. If they get leggy, you may need to move them to a sunnier location or supplement them with a grow light. When the weather is nice and the plants are 3 to 4 inches (7.5 to 10 cm) high, it's time to harden them off. Place them in a sheltered but sunny outdoor spot, starting by leaving them out just an hour or two and easing them into staying outside all day; bring them in at night. Do this over the course of a week. Once they've acclimated, plant them outdoors in a container, raised bed, or straight into the ground.

HAPPY
SEEDLING

HUNGRY
SEEDLING

USDA ZONES

The USDA hardiness zones are based off the average annual low temperatures, and help you to determine what plants will thrive in your region.

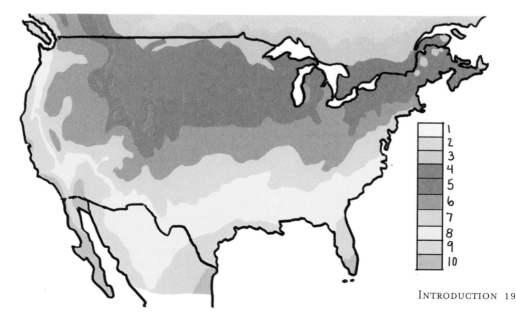

YOUR HERB GARDEN

Sometimes it's best to start small and ease your way into planting a full garden. Here are some of my favorite herbs to get you started.

ROSEMARY

Perennials that thrive in full sun and dry, well-drained soil. Will grow into a large bush with lovely purple flowers.

CILANTRO/ CORIANDER

Annuals that need full sun and 12 inches (30.5 cm) of well-drained soil.

SAGE

Needs full sun and well-drained soil. Usually an annual but can be grown as a perennial in temperate climates. It grows well in containers.

CHIVES

Chives are easy-to-grow perennials that thrive in light shade to full sun.

PARSLEY

Biennials that prefer full sun to light shade. Parsley is very successful in pots.

THYME

This perennial needs full sun and dry, sandy soil.

OREGANO

Perennials that need full sun. Perfect for containers because they need well-drained soil.

MARJORAM

Needs full sun and well-drained soil. Does very well in containers.

BASIL

Needs full sun. Plant directly in the ground or in a pot at least 12 inches (30.5 cm) deep.

HOW TO PICK AND PREPARE HERBS

For herbs with woody stems like mint, tarragon, rosemary, thyme, oregano, and marjoram, don't pick the leaves off one by one. Gently pinch the stem with your thumb and forefinger and pull the leaves off as you slide your fingers down the stem.

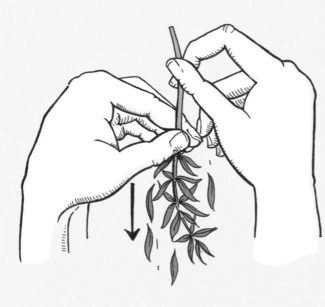

For herbs with delicate stems like cilantro, basil, and parsley, begin by chopping off and discarding the thicker stems, then chop the leaves and tender stems together.

EQUAL DAY & NIGHT

SPR

Spring is my favorite season; it promises warmth, more light, and fresh starts. Spring is the time to get your hands dirty and get your garden started. I love to go shopping for seeds and figure out what vegetables I want to plant for the coming months. Starting seedlings indoors (see page 18) brings new life into your home. It's just so lovely and homey to have all my seedlings sprouting on the windowsills.

This season's recipes capture the qualities that I like most about spring: crisp flavors, colorful produce, and all-around freshness. Make them on their own or as part of a full spring meal to bring the outside in.

WHAT IS IN SEASON IN
SPRING
FAVA BEANS
ASPARAGUS
SUGAR SNAP PEAS
RADISHES
SPINACH
BLUEBERRIES

BEANS

HOW TO GROW FAVA BEANS

Fava beans grow best in moist soil that is 60° to 65°F (16° to 18°C). In the northern United States and Canada, plant the beans as early as the soil can be worked. Fava beans actually germinate well in cool soil, and the plants can tolerate temperatures as low as 15°F (-9°C). In areas with a mild winter, such as the Pacific Northwest and the South, fava beans can even be planted in the late fall or winter for an early spring crop.

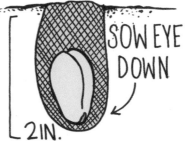

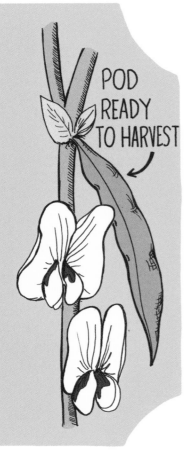

When you're ready to plant, sow your seeds eye down, 1 to 2 inches (2.5 to 5 cm) deep and 4 inches (10 cm) apart. When they're about 2 inches (5 cm) high, thin them to every 8 inches (20 cm). The plants will grow 2 to 4 feet (61 to 122 cm) tall, so they should be staked while they're young—a strong wind could ruin plants that are heavy with beans.

Harvest the pods when they're about 6 inches (15 cm) long. They should look full but not over-bulging. Once the weather warms up, aphids could become a problem; blast them off with a strong spray of water, or snap off and discard the sections of the plant where the bugs congregate.

HOW TO PEEL FAVA BEANS

1. SNAP OFF THE TOP OF THE POD & PULL BACK THE STRING. SEPARATE THE TWO HALVES OF THE POD. REMOVE THE BEANS FROM THE POD.

2. BRING A POT OF WATER TO A BOIL & PREPARE AN ICE BATH.

3. BLANCH THE BEANS FOR 30 SECONDS. DRAIN, THEN SUBMERGE THEM IN THE ICE BATH TO HALT COOKING.

4. GIVE THE BEANS A SQUEEZE TO POP THEM OUT OF THEIR WHITISH SHELLS. DON'T SQUEEZE THE BEANS SO HARD THAT YOU SMASH THEM. IF THEY DON'T POP RIGHT OUT, PEEL BACK THE SHELL WITH A PARING KNIFE.

FAVA BEAN

CROSTINI

SERVES 4 TO 6

Shelling fava beans certainly takes some effort, but their buttery texture and nutty flavor are worth the trouble. Once the fava beans are shelled, this appetizer comes together quickly and maximizes your efforts, literally spreading the reward around. The nuttiness of the fava beans is complemented by the clean, crisp flavors of the lemon juice and mint, and the crunch of the toast adds a great contrast to the soft spread. If you're planning a dinner party, you can shell the beans the night before and the whole thing can be prepared in 15 minutes. You can substitute lima beans or edamame for the favas if you'd like.

BAGUETTE, SLICED ON THE BIAS

1/4 CUP (60 ML) PLUS 1 TO 2 TABLESPOONS OLIVE OIL

1 CLOVE GARLIC

1 CUP SHELLED FAVA BEANS (1 1/4 POUNDS/570 G IN SHELL)

4 TEASPOONS LEMON JUICE

1/4 TEASPOON GRATED LEMON ZEST

1/2 TEASPOON SALT

MINT LEAVES FOR GARNISH (1 PER TOAST)

PARMESAN CHEESE, SHAVED (ABOUT 2 OUNCES/55 G)

ABOUT 45°

SLICE ON THE BIAS.

BLEND TOGETHER.

Preheat the oven to 400°F (205°C). Arrange the baguette slices in a single layer on a baking sheet and drizzle them with the 1 to 2 tablespoons oil. Slice the clove of garlic lengthwise and rub the cut side all over the top of the bread slices. Put it aside. Toast the bread in the oven for 9 to 10 minutes, until golden. Peel the fava beans from their outer shell following the instructions on page 29. Put the fava beans, the remaining 1/4 cup (60 ml) oil, the lemon juice, lemon zest, garlic, and salt in a food processor. Pulse until you have a mixture that is blended but still has a little texture (it shouldn't be completely smooth like hummus). Put a healthy dollop of the fava mixture on each piece of toast. Top with some cheese and a mint leaf and serve.

TOP WITH SHAVED PARMESAN.

HOW TO GROW ASPARAGUS

Asparagus is one of my favorite vegetables. It's so versatile and has the most wonderful vegetal flavor. Asparagus gardening is a commitment, and best for folks who don't move often. It requires a dedicated spot in your garden and it takes a few years before your first harvest, but the same plants will provide you with asparagus for twenty years or longer.

Asparagus is a perennial, and the part we eat is actually the young shoots that come up in the spring. After a few weeks of harvesting the shoots, the asparagus plant grows into tall stalks with ferny leaves. Asparagus grows well in most areas, except places with exceptionally mild winters, because the plants need cold weather to go dormant.

**SHOOTS
(THE TASTY PART)**

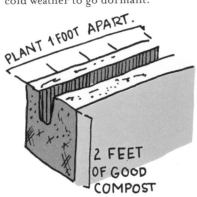

PLANT 1 FOOT APART.

2 FEET
OF GOOD
COMPOST

Because you need to provide the plants with enough nutrients for many years, you have to prepare your garden bed carefully. Pick a spot in direct sunlight, remove all roots and weeds, and dig in 2 feet (61 cm) of manure and compost. You will need to plant 10 to 12 plants per person (if you really love asparagus, or plan to can some, plant more than this).

**FULL-GROWN
PLANT
(NOT TASTY)**

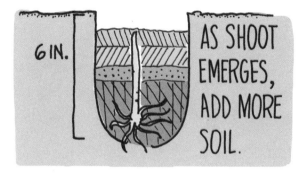

6 IN.

AS SHOOT EMERGES, ADD MORE SOIL.

Plant asparagus plants 1 foot (30.5 cm) apart in the bed you prepared by digging a trench 1 foot (30.5 cm) wide and 6 inches (15 cm) deep and placing year-old crowns at the bottom. Cover them with 3 inches (7.5 cm) of dirt. As the shoots emerge, cover with more dirt until the trench is full.

The plants need regular watering for the first two years. During the third year, you can harvest your spears, but only for about a month. After the third year, your harvest can be extended to two months. Harvest the shoots every other day by cutting or breaking the shoot right at dirt level. When your harvest period has ended, let your plants grow tall and ferny. After the foliage has turned brown in the winter, you can cut the plants down for the next year. In the coldest areas, wait until spring to cut them, as the dead foliage protects the crowns.

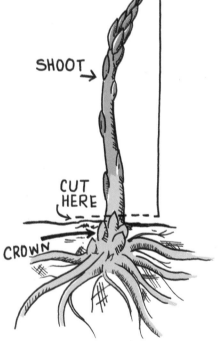

SHOOT

CUT HERE

CROWN

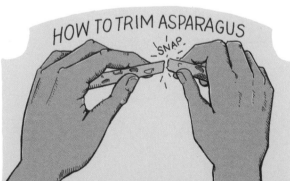

HOW TO TRIM ASPARAGUS

SNAP.

To trim asparagus, grip each end of the spear between your thumb and forefinger and snap the spear in half. It will naturally break where the tender (edible) part meets the woody end.

ASPARAGUS SOUP

With Crème Fraîche

SERVES 4 TO 6

The first time I made this soup, I knew I had done a good thing. It's light, fresh, and tastes like spring. It brings the best of the vegetal flavors forward, and the lemon imparts a bright element. This soup makes a great light meal or starter course. If you're enjoying it as a meal, serve with crusty bread and white wine for a real treat.

4 CUPS (960 ML) VEGETABLE BROTH

I POUND (455 G) ASPARAGUS, TRIMMED AND
    CHOPPED (RESERVE WOODY ENDS)

3 TABLESPOONS OLIVE OIL

4 CLOVES GARLIC, MINCED

3 SMALL LEEKS, WHITE AND LIGHT GREEN PARTS,
    CHOPPED AND WASHED

2 TABLESPOONS ALL-PURPOSE FLOUR

1 1/2 TEASPOONS SALT

1/2 TEASPOON FRESHLY GROUND BLACK PEPPER

1/4 CUP (60 ML) LEMON JUICE

HOMEMADE CRÈME FRAÎCHE (SEE PAGE 38)

LIGHT, FRESH FLAVORS.

SIMMER ENDS
IN BROTH.

Put the broth and woody asparagus ends in a small saucepan. Simmer for 15 minutes, to infuse the broth with asparagus flavor. While the broth simmers, heat the oil in a large pot, add the garlic and leeks, and sauté over medium heat for 10 minutes. Add the flour and stir continuously for 2 minutes to make a light roux. Remove the woody stems from the broth with a slotted spoon and discard them. Pour the broth into the large pot with the leeks and garlic. Add the raw asparagus and simmer for 10 minutes, or until the asparagus is bright green and tender. (Don't cook it so long that it becomes dark and mushy.) Remove from the heat, and with an immersion blender or in an upright blender, puree in small batches until completely smooth. Season with salt and pepper and stir in the lemon juice. Serve with a dollop of crème fraîche (see page 38).

STIR IN LEMON JUICE.

HOMEMADE CRÈME FRAÎCHE

Crème fraîche sounds like a fancy gourmet item, but it's really just a milder version of sour cream. It's easy to make and tastes great stirred into soups, eaten with berries, or dolloped on French toast. In this very simple fermentation process, you inoculate heavy cream and then let it sit at room temperature. The bacteria cultures thicken the cream and make it slightly tangy.

1 CUP WHIPPING CREAM
1 TABLESPOON YOGURT OR BUTTERMILK

Gently warm the cream to about 100°F (38°C). Stir in the yogurt to inoculate the cream with live active cultures. Pour into a clean jar and cover with a clean dishtowel, using a rubber band to secure the cloth in place. Set in a warm place, such as the back of the stove, for 12 to 24 hours, or until the cream has thickened. Put a lid on the jar, refrigerate, and use within 10 days.

SUGAR
SNAP
PEAS

HOW TO GROW SUGAR SNAP PEAS

Legumes, such as peas, are an important part of crop rotation in your garden, because they release nitrogen back into the soil (see page 16). Growing sugar snap peas is easy and rewarding regardless of your space constraints. If you have a larger garden, peas are quick to grow and make for an attractive accent as they work their way up the trellis. If you're short on space, there are bush varieties as well, which are able to stand on their own and do well in containers.

To encourage the seeds to germinate, soak them in water overnight before planting, and plant each seed about 1 inch (2.5 cm) deep in the soil. For bush varieties, space the seeds 6 inches (15 cm) apart, and thin to one plant every foot. Vine varieties can be planted as close together as ½ inch (12 mm), but they need plenty of room to grow up.

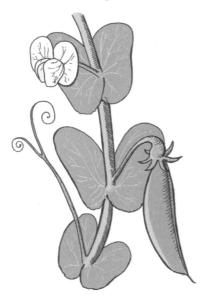

A sturdy trellis 6 feet (1.8 m) high should do the trick—put the trellis in place before you sow. You should plant the peas straight into the soil where they'll be staying; they have delicate root systems that don't do well when transplanted. Sow the seeds a few weeks before the last frost.

Harvest the peas when they start to fatten. Regular harvesting will keep the plants producing peas, so make time to pick them almost every day. Peas have the best flavor right after picking because their sugars begin to turn to starch after a few hours, so plan to use them the day you pick them. Once the temperature reaches 80°F (27°C), the plants will stop producing. Once they stop producing, trim them back to soil level, leaving the roots to decompose, which will release the nitrogen back into the soil.

RADISHES

Radishes are another quick-growing spring crop, and they require full sun and well-drained soil. Sow the seeds into loosened soil two weeks before the last spring frost, and do successive plantings every week until early summer. Radishes grow very quickly, and some varieties are ready for harvest only three weeks after they're sown. Radishes taste best if they have plenty of moisture, so make sure to mulch over the plants to keep weeds down and moisture in. Pull the radishes up as soon as the roots are mature.

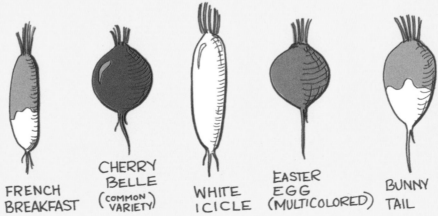

FRENCH BREAKFAST

CHERRY BELLE (COMMON VARIETY)

WHITE ICICLE

EASTER EGG (MULTICOLORED)

BUNNY TAIL

SUGAR SNAP PEA
~ AND ~
# PEA

RADISH SALAD

SERVES 4 TO 6

This beautifully simple salad highlights the best qualities of spring produce. It is fresh, wonderfully crunchy, and full of gorgeous colors. The sweetness of the peas and honey is perfectly complemented by the peppery spice of the radishes. It makes a great side dish for dinner or a perfect springtime lunch.

2 TABLESPOONS LEMON JUICE

¹/2 TEASPOON DIJON MUSTARD

¹/4 CUP (60 ML) OLIVE OIL

¹/2 TEASPOON HONEY

¹/4 TEASPOON SALT PLUS MORE FOR SPRINKLING, IF DESIRED

3 CUPS (190 G) SUGAR SNAP PEAS, CUT IN HALF

I CUP (110 G) RADISHES, THINLY SLICED

¹/2 CUP (60 G) CRUMBLED FETA CHEESE

FRESHLY GROUND BLACK PEPPER TO TASTE (OPTIONAL)

To make the dressing, first whisk together the lemon juice and mustard in a small bowl. Slowly add the oil by whisking it in drop by drop to emulsify it with the lemon juice. As it begins to incorporate, you can increase the rate to a slow stream. This can easily be done with a food processor or handheld immersion blender as well. After the oil is incorporated, whisk in the honey and salt. In a large bowl, combine the peas, radishes, and cheese. Toss with the dressing, top with a sprinkle of salt and pepper, if desired, and serve.

HOW TO GROW SPINACH

Spinach is a crop ideally suited to cooler, early spring weather, and it thrives in places with a long, mild spring. In places with a shorter spring, spinach can be planted in the shade of taller crops to extend the harvest. Sow your seeds as soon as the soil can be worked, or up to 6 weeks before the last expected frost. In areas with a mild winter, you can plant in February to begin harvesting in March.

PLANT 2 IN. APART

THIN SEEDLINGS TO 6 IN.

GIVE MATURE PLANTS 12 IN.

12 INCHES OF LOOSE, FERTILE SOIL

Prepare your bed by loosening 12 inches (30.5 cm) of the soil and plant the seeds ½ inch (12 mm) deep and 2 inches (5 cm) apart, thinning to one plant every 6 inches (15 cm) once the seedlings are established (but don't toss the baby greens—enjoy the small tender leaves in a salad!). Stagger your planting by sowing a row every 10 days for fresh spinach all through the spring. Heat, lack of water, and overcrowding will cause spinach to quickly bolt (produce flowers and seeds), so keep the soil moist to keep the plant cool. Harvest spinach after 4 to 6 weeks, when the leaves look big enough to eat. Heat will turn the leaves bitter, so harvest your plants before the temperature reaches 80°F (27°C). Carefully cut the outer leaves of the plant and leave the rest to be able to continue harvesting from the same plant. When it looks like it's close to bolting, cut the whole plant.

SPINACH GONE TO SEED

HARVEST OUTER LEAVES FIRST

PLANT IN THE SHADE OF TALL PLANTS TO EXTEND HARVEST.

SPINACH & MUSHROOM
LASAGNA

SERVES 6 TO 8

Generally, if I'm eating pasta I want it with red sauce. However, when I discovered béchamel sauce my mind was forever changed. Béchamel is one of the mother sauces in French cooking, and it's pretty darn tasty in a lasagna. It allows the mushrooms and the spinach to shine, where tomato sauce would overpower their more delicate flavors. The absence of ricotta makes this lasagna rich without being overly decadent—perfect for a spring dinner.

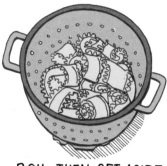

BOIL, THEN SET ASIDE.

¹/2 TEASPOON OLIVE OIL

I TEASPOON SALT

I2 LASAGNA NOODLES

4 CUPS (960 ML) WHOLE MILK

8 TABLESPOONS (I STICK/II5 G) UNSALTED BUTTER,
    CUT INTO I-INCH (2.5-CM) CUBES

¹/3 CUP (40 G) ALL-PURPOSE FLOUR

¹/2 TEASPOON FRESHLY GRATED NUTMEG

2 CLOVES GARLIC, MINCED

I POUND (455 G) MUSHROOMS, THINLY SLICED

I POUND (455 G) SPINACH

I ¹/2 CUPS (I80 G) GRATED PARMESAN CHEESE

WHISK CONSTANTLY.

Preheat the oven to 400°F (205°C). Put the oil and ½ teaspoon of the salt in a large pot of water and bring to a boil. Add the lasagna noodles and boil for 10 minutes, stirring occasionally. Drain and set aside. While the pasta cooks, warm the milk in a saucepan over low heat to 100°F (38°C) and set it aside. In a large saucepan over low heat, melt 6 tablespoons (85 g) of the butter. Once the foam dissipates, stir in the flour and whisk constantly for at least 3 minutes, or until the mixture begins to brown. Slowly add the warmed milk, whisking in a little at a time. Once you've stirred in half the milk, you can add the rest all at once. While stirring constantly, heat until the mixture is thick but still pourable. Remove it from heat and mix in the remaining ½ teaspoon salt and the nutmeg. Set the béchamel aside. [CONT.]

In a separate large pot, melt 1 tablespoon of the butter over medium heat. Add the garlic, a dash of salt, and about half the mushrooms and sauté until they begin releasing their juices, about 3 minutes. Add the remaining 1 tablespoon butter and the remaining mushrooms. After a few minutes, begin adding the spinach a few handfuls at a time. Continue adding as it wilts down. Remove from the heat when all the spinach is wilted.

THINLY SLICE.

Pour enough béchamel to cover the bottom of a 9-by-13-inch (23-by-33-cm) glass casserole dish and spread to coat. Cover with three noodles, side by side, and trim any overlap. Spread more sauce on top of the noodles, and spoon in one third of the spinach and mushroom mixture. Spread evenly. Sprinkle on one quarter of the cheese. Repeat this process two more times, finishing with a layer of noodles, the remaining sauce, and the remaining cheese. Bake, uncovered, for 30 to 35 minutes, until golden and bubbly. Serve.

- SAUCE
- NOODLES
- VEGGIES
- CHEESE

HOW TO GROW BLUEBERRIES

Blueberries are a native species to the United States and thrive in many parts of the country. The key to growing them successfully is to find a variety that is suited for your region. The main varieties of blueberries are highbush, lowbush, and rabbiteye.

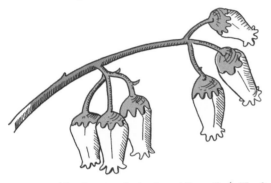

LOWBUSH

12 TO 24 IN.

Blueberries thrive in acidic soils (pH of 4.5 to 5.5), but if your area's soil has a higher pH, or you don't have a lot of grow room, you can grow them in large containers on your patio. To get nonacidic soil to the proper pH level, you should dig a deep hole and fill it with equal parts peat moss and sand, then mulch with untreated aged sawdust before you plant your bush. Plant the bushes about 5 feet (1.5 m) apart and mulch about 3 inches (7.5 cm) deep to keep plants moist.

6 TO 12 FEET

HIGHBUSH

SHAKE!

Blueberries are ripe from mid-May through June. You'll know they're ready when they come off the bush with a light touch. Protect your crop by covering it with bird-proof netting. (Birds love blueberries and will eat your entire crop!)

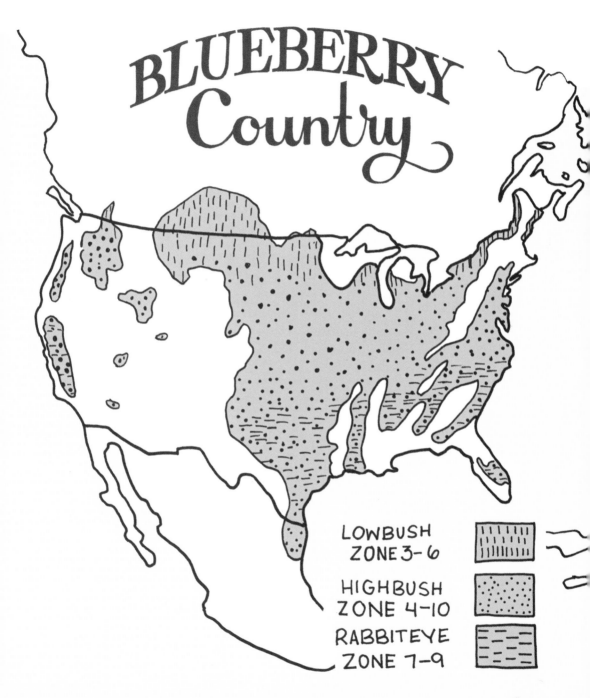

BLUEBERRY Country

LOWBUSH
ZONE 3-6

HIGHBUSH
ZONE 4-10

RABBITEYE
ZONE 7-9

SERVES 8 TO 10

This cake is for those of you who find yourselves with a bumper crop of blueberries—whether you've grown your own or bought a gallon bag of pie berries from the farmers' market. This dense, moist cake puts them front and center. If there's any left over, it also makes a great breakfast treat the next day!

---

1 1/2 CUPS (170 G) ALL-PURPOSE FLOUR

1/2 CUP (70 G) CORNMEAL

1/2 TEASPOONS BAKING POWDER

1/2 TEASPOON BAKING SODA

1/2 TEASPOON SALT

9 TABLESPOONS (125 G) UNSALTED BUTTER, SOFTENED

1/2 CUP (120 ML) PLUS 2 TABLESPOONS MAPLE SYRUP, PREFERABLY GRADE A DARK AMBER (SEE PAGE 55)

2 EGGS

2/3 CUP (165 ML) PLAIN WHOLE-MILK YOGURT

1 TEASPOON VANILLA EXTRACT

3 CUPS (504 G) BLUEBERRIES

1/2 CUP (40 G) ROLLED OATS

1/2 CUP (50 G) PECANS

PIE BERRIES
(MIX OF UNDER & OVER RIPE FRUIT)

GREASE & FLOUR.

Preheat the oven to 325°F (165°C). Grease and flour a 10-inch (25-cm) round cake pan and set aside. Mix together the flour, cornmeal, baking powder, baking soda, and salt in a large bowl. In a separate bowl, cream 8 tablespoons (112 g) of the butter and the ½ cup (120 ml) syrup with an electric mixer on medium speed, about 3 minutes. Mix in the eggs, yogurt, and vanilla. Mix the wet ingredients into the dry, one half at a time. Fold the blueberries into the batter with a spatula and pour it into the cake pan. In a separate bowl, mix the oats, pecans, the remaining 1 tablespoon butter, and the remaining 2 tablespoons syrup to make the crumble. Spread it evenly over the top of the cake batter. Bake for 55 minutes, or until a knife inserted into the center comes out clean. Serve with whipped cream (see page 54).

FOLD IN BERRIES.

Whipped Cream

Whipped cream is one of those things that is just too simple to buy readymade. Plus, homemade tastes so much better! I never knew whipped cream beyond Cool Whip until I was an adult. The effort-to-rewards ratio is pretty high on this one, folks. Once you try fresh, you'll never go back to "whipped dairy products."

1 CUP WHIPPING CREAM
½ TEASPOON VANILLA
3 TABLESPOONS POWDERED SUGAR

Before you start, make sure the cream, the bowl, and whisk are cold. If you have time, put the bowl and the whisk in the freezer for a few minutes beforehand. In a large bowl, start whisking the cream either by hand using large strokes in different directions, or with an electric mixer on medium speed. When soft peaks begin to form, add the vanilla and powdered sugar. Continue whisking until the peaks return and can stand on their own.

BAKING WITH SWEETENERS

Unless you're baking a delicate cake or pastry, try substituting unrefined sweeteners in your recipe. You can replace granulated sugar with maple syrup or honey in most recipes. Use ¾ cup maple syrup or honey for every 1 cup granulated sugar. When baking with maple syrup or honey, reduce the liquid in the recipe by 3 tablespoons for every cup used and reduce the oven temperature by 25°F to avoid burning. Maple syrup and honey can be used interchangeably.

GUIDE TO MAPLE SYRUP

The grading system for maple syrup doesn't have to do with quality but rather the color and flavor.

GRADE A LIGHT AMBER
Light, delicate flavor is best used as a topping.

GRADE A MEDIUM AMBER
Slightly deeper flavor, still good as a topping, provides a mild maple flavor for baking.

GRADE A DARK AMBER
Very strong flavor, a little too deep for some to use as a syrup, works well for baking.

GRADE B
Very dark color and deep robust flavor, best used for baking. The flavor may be too strong for some to be used as a topping.

Summer is when your garden is in full swing, and the easiest time of the year to eat fresh. The farmers' markets are full of fresh produce, and the long days give us plenty of light for dinner outside. I grew up in North Carolina, where the sweltering summers were a time for sipping iced tea in the shade and trying not to move around too much. By contrast, Bay Area summers are cool and foggy. There are many microclimates around the bay, and some aren't sunny enough for the most heat-loving vegetables. For instance, Berkeley, where I live, has afternoons that are warm enough for smaller tomatoes, but large heirloom varieties just don't ripen for me. Our summers are cool and refreshing, but, truthfully, I miss the hot summers of my childhood.

The recipes for this season hit the highlights of summer produce for a variety of climates. Vine-ripened tomatoes, corn, watermelon, and berries take center stage in these produce-forward dishes. There's no reason to resort to canned or frozen fruits and veggies this time of year.

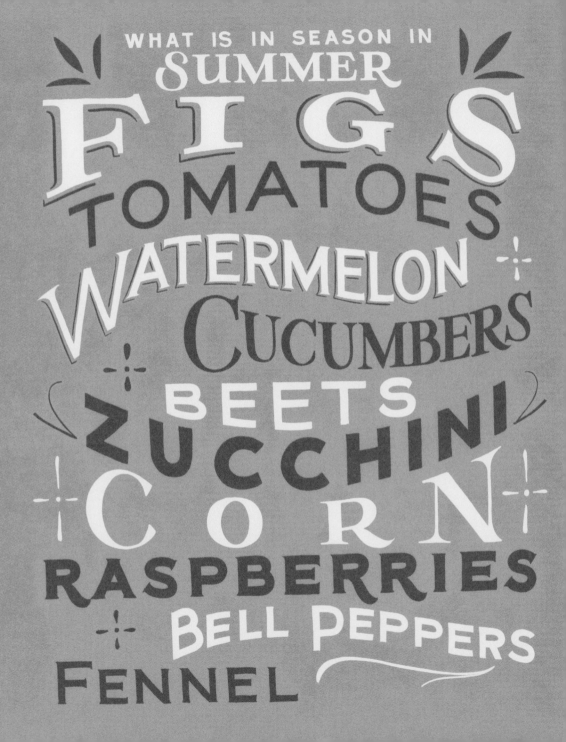

HOW TO GROW FIGS

Figs are semihardy trees that grow well in warm climates. Though figs will grow in most parts of the Southeast and on the West Coast (zones 8 to 10), it's important to select the cultivar best suited to your area.

Figs produce two crops of fruit a year, one in early summer and one in late summer. An established tree will yield 25 to 30 pounds (11 to 14 kg) of fruit per year. In areas where the temperature gets below 15°F (-9°C), you can plant figs in a large

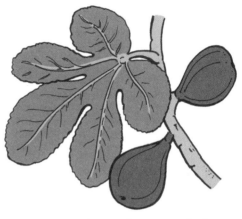

GROW IN CONTAINERS IN ZONES 6 TO 7.

container and move them into a shed or garage for the winter. Choose a sunny spot with southern exposure for your tree. Don't overwater or overfertilize it. Harvest the figs when they're soft and fall easily into your hand. If they ooze white sap when you try to pick them, they're not ripe yet.

BLACK MISSION
GROWS WELL IN CALIFORNIA

CELESTE
GROWS WELL IN THE SOUTH

BROWN TURKEY
MORE COLD TOLERANT

KING
GROWS WELL IN THE N.WEST

SERVES 6 TO 8

This is a simple appetizer that comes together very quickly. Fresh figs are a thing of beauty, and the gorgonzola and honey accompany but don't overpower the delicate figs.

12 RIPE FIGS

3 OUNCES (90 G) CRUMBLED GORGONZOLA CHEESE

¼ CUP (85 G) HONEY (CHOOSE A LIGHT FLORAL
    HONEY, LIKE CLOVER)

Preheat the broiler. Slice each fig in half lengthwise. Place the figs cut side up in a baking pan. Divide the gorgonzola evenly among the figs, placing a chunk on top of each. Put the pan under the broiler for 5 minutes, until the figs are warm and the cheese is melted. Drizzle the honey over the figs and serve.

NOTE:

Try wrapping the grilled fig with a small, thin slice of prosciutto, securing it with a toothpick. It really steps up the flavor.

SLICE IN HALF.

DRIZZLE WITH HONEY.

BEE FRIENDLY

Bees are vital to our food system: One-third of all the food we eat is pollinated by bees. Unfortunately, bees (both honeybees and native species) have been struggling over the last several years because of "colony collapse disorder." If you're interested in helping the honeybees, you might consider taking up beekeeping! It helps the environment, helps our gardens, and if you're good to your bees, you'll be rewarded with gallons of honey every spring. If you don't feel up to the task of keeping bees, consider keeping a bee-friendly garden instead. Keep it full of pesticide-free flowering plants, including ones native to your area.

WORKER BEE

TOMATOES

HOW TO GROW TOMATOES

There are many varieties of tomatoes, so make sure to select one that's well suited to your climate, or try growing multiple varieties to extend the harvest. Tomatoes do best when started indoors; I recommend starting them 6 to 8 weeks before the last frost in your area.

To begin, sprinkle seeds over the entire surface of a flat that's 3 inches (7.5 cm) deep, then cover with ¼ inch (6 mm) of soil. Place the flat in a window that will receive plenty of sun, and keep the soil moist. When the seedlings' first true leaves appear, transplant the strongest plants into individual cups or pots that have drainage holes. Plant the seedling on its side so more roots grow down from the stem.

PLANT THE SEEDLING ON ITS SIDE. MORE ROOTS WILL GROW FROM THE STEM.

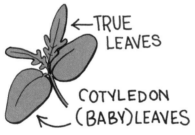

←TRUE LEAVES

COTYLEDON (BABY)LEAVES

When the threat of frost has passed, slowly start hardening off your seedlings (see page 19). Only plant the strongest seedlings in your garden. When you're ready to plant, dig a hole and bury them up to their "armpits," where the lowest leaves meet the stem.

There are two types of tomatoes: determinate and indeterminate (this will be indicated on your seed packet). Determinate plants are bush varieties and should be planted 2 feet (61 cm) apart. Indeterminate varieties will grow long vines. You can bury a 6-foot (1.8-m) stake next to the small plant and train it up the stake as it grows, or you can plant them 3 to 4 feet (.9 to 1.2 m) apart and let the vines run all over the place.

SMALL GREEN TOMATO

I find the easiest way to grow the indeterminate variety is to make a round cage with chicken wire around your stake and contain the growth within. Make sure to add mulch to keep in moisture and smother weeds. Regularly harvest the ripe fruits by cutting or gently twisting them off the vine. Tomatoes do well in containers and can easily be planted on sunny patios. Don't let a small space stop you from enjoying fresh summer tomatoes!

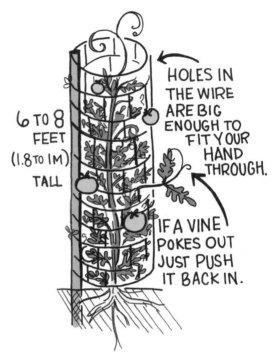

6 TO 8 FEET (1.8 TO 1M) TALL

HOLES IN THE WIRE ARE BIG ENOUGH TO FIT YOUR HAND THROUGH.

IF A VINE POKES OUT JUST PUSH IT BACK IN.

WHAT DOES HEIRLOOM MEAN?

Heirloom plants are openly pollinated cultivars whose seeds have been passed down for generations. Heirloom plants have been allowed to cross naturally, instead of being manually crossed like hybrid plants (hybrids don't "reproduce true," meaning you can't save their seeds with reliable results). Heirlooms have more genetic variation, and over time gardeners save the seeds from the strongest plants, best adapted to their climate. Heirloom doesn't mean more "natural" than hybrid, just that you can reliably save the vegetables' seeds for the next season. The only unnatural seeds are those that are GMOs, or genetically modified organisms, which have had their genes spliced together in a lab rather than by pollination.

Heirloom tomatoes come in a wide range of colors, shapes, and sizes. I think they're fun to grow because of the gorgeous variety, and they have great taste and texture. Most heirloom tomatoes are indeterminate, meaning they grow on long vines. If you have a small growing space, I would stick with hybrid bush varieties.

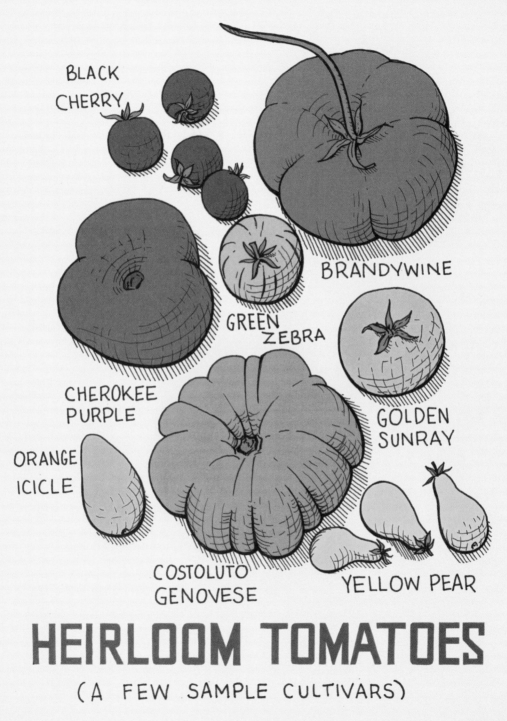

BLACK CHERRY

BRANDYWINE

GREEN ZEBRA

CHEROKEE PURPLE

GOLDEN SUNRAY

ORANGE ICICLE

COSTOLUTO GENOVESE

YELLOW PEAR

HEIRLOOM TOMATOES

(A FEW SAMPLE CULTIVARS)

HOW TO PEEL AND SEED A TOMATO

1. CORE THE TOMATO BY CUTTING OUT A WEDGE AROUND THE STEM. REMOVE THE STEM & THE CORE.

2. CUT AN "X" IN THE BOTTOM.

3. FILL A LARGE POT WITH ENOUGH WATER TO COVER THE TOMATOES & BRING TO A BOIL.

4. INDIVIDUALLY BOIL EACH TOMATO FOR 30 SECONDS.

5. REMOVE THE TOMATO FROM THE WATER WITH A SLOTTED SPOON & SLIP THE SKIN OFF.

6. CUT THE TOMATO IN HALF AT ITS EQUATOR & SQUEEZE THE SEEDS OUT OVER A SINK OR BOWL. PICK OUT ANY REMAINING SEEDS WITH YOUR FINGERS.

SAVE YOUR SEEDS

IF YOU'RE GROWING HEIRLOOM
TOMATOES, CONTINUE THE
TRADITION & SAVE YOUR
SEEDS FOR NEXT YEAR.

1. CHOOSE A FULLY RIPE
TOMATO, FROM A HEALTHY
PLANT. SLICE IT IN HALF
& SQUEEZE THE SEEDS
INTO A SMALL GLASS. STIR
IN 2 TABLESPOONS OF WATER.

2. SET ASIDE IN A DARK
SPOT FOR 3 TO 4 DAYS. MOLD
WILL PROBABLY GROW.

3. SCRAPE OFF THE MOLD,
ADD ½ CUP (120 ML) WATER
& STIR. THE GOOD SEEDS
WILL SINK. CAREFULLY
POUR OFF FLOATING PULP &
BAD SEEDS. REPEAT.

4. DRAIN SEEDS & SPREAD
THEM ON A COFFEE FILTER
OR PAPER PLATE. DON'T
USE A PAPER TOWEL—THE
SEEDS WILL STICK TO IT.

5. AFTER SEVERAL DAYS
OF DRYING, STORE THEM
IN AN AIRTIGHT CONTAINER.

SQUEEZE OUT
SEEDS.

2 TBS.
WATER

TBS   TBS

A
LITTLE
MOLD
IS
OKAY.

← BAD
SEEDS
FLOAT

← GOOD
SEEDS
SINK

DRY
ON A
COFFEE
FILTER

SERVES 4 TO 6

This summer soup is cool and refreshing and takes advantage of the bounty of summer. The twist on traditional gazpacho is that watermelon serves as the broth. The melon base makes it slightly sweet, but the savory ingredients make it more of a soup and less like an agua fresca. It's light but satisfying, the best kind of dish for the hottest of summer days.

I CUP (185 G) PEELED AND SEEDED TOMATOES (SEE PAGE 68)

5 CUPS (760 G) CUBED WATERMELON, SEEDS REMOVED

I YELLOW BELL PEPPER, ROUGHLY CHOPPED

I MEDIUM CUCUMBER, PEELED AND ROUGHLY CHOPPED

I CLOVE GARLIC, MINCED

2 TABLESPOONS MINCED RED ONION

I TEASPOON SALT

1/2 TEASPOON FRESHLY GROUND BLACK PEPPER

2 TABLESPOONS RED WINE VINEGAR

2 TABLESPOONS CHOPPED FRESH BASIL

1/3 CUP (75 ML) OLIVE OIL

USE PERFECT PRODUCE.

Combine the tomatoes, watermelon, bell pepper, cucumber, garlic, and onion in a large bowl. Use an immersion blender to puree until mostly smooth. Add the salt, black pepper, vinegar, and basil and continue to puree. Slowly add the oil in a steady stream while the blender is running. Cover and chill. Serve cold.

COMBINE & PUREE.

WATERMELONS

Watermelons do best in areas with sandy soil and long, hot, dry summers. Sow soon after the soil has warmed to 60°F (16°C), so there's plenty of time for the melons to ripen in the summer heat. While the vines are growing, watermelons need a lot of water at their roots. Plenty of mulch will help retain moisture and keep the roots warm. Once the fruit starts to ripen, cut back on the irrigation so it doesn't dilute the sugars in the fruit. You can tell if your watermelon is ripe by thumping the melon; listen for a dull hollow sound. Unripe watermelons say "pink," while ripe watermelons say "punk."

CHECK ITS BELLY

& GIVE IT A THUMP.

PUNK

WITHERED TENDRIL

THAT'S A RIPE MELON!

CUCUMBERS

Cucumbers are warm-weather plants that need heat and plenty of water to thrive. There are bush and vine varieties of cucumbers. The seeds should be planted a least 2 weeks after the last expected frost. If temperatures are projected to be under 70°F (21°C) for a while, you can use a row cover or heavy mulch to keep plants warm (a cheap and easy cover for a baby cucumber plant is a plastic milk jug with the cap removed and the bottom cut off!). Harvest often and keep the soil evenly moist to prevent bitter fruit.

BEETS

HOW TO GROW BEETS

Beets grow best in well-drained soil that's deep, loose, and rock free. Sow them in a sunny spot 3 to 4 weeks before your last expected frost. For a continual harvest, continue to sow every 2 weeks until daytime temperatures reach about 75°F (24°C). Soak the seeds overnight before planting to ensure successful germination. Then begin sowing again 8 weeks before first frost.

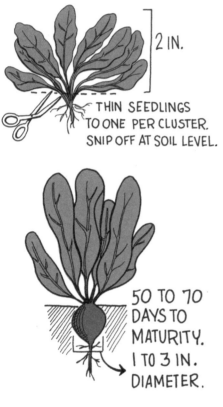

2 IN.

THIN SEEDLINGS TO ONE PER CLUSTER. SNIP OFF AT SOIL LEVEL.

50 TO 70 DAYS TO MATURITY. 1 TO 3 IN. DIAMETER.

Plant each seed directly into the ground, ½ inch (12 mm) deep, 3 inches (7.5 cm) apart. Rows should be 12 to 18 inches (30.5 to 46 cm) apart. Each seed actually contains 2 to 6 seeds within, so you will definitely have to thin your seedlings. When the seedlings are about 2 inches (5 cm) high, thin each bunch, leaving the strongest-looking plants. Use scissors to snip off the leaves of the plants you are culling, as pulling them up will damage the root system of the plant you want to save—you can use these microgreens in a salad!

Beets require moisture, so don't let them dry out. Mulching helps keep the soil moist. It takes 50 to 70 days for the plants to reach maturity. You can harvest beets once they've reached 1 to 3 inches (2.5 to 7.5 cm) in diameter; be sure to harvest before they get too big, as they get tough and woody if they grow bigger than 4 inches (10 cm) in diameter. Cut off the tops, leaving 1 to 2 inches (2.5 to 5 cm) of stem, and store unwashed until you're ready to use them.

ALBINO   CHIOGGIA   BULL'S BLOOD   GOLDEN

HOW TO ROAST BEETS

1. SLICE THE GREENS OFF, LEAVING
   ABOUT 1-INCH OF STEM.
   SCRUB THE BEETS CLEAN.

2. PLACE THE BEETS ON PARCHMENT
   PAPER—LINED ALUMINUM FOIL
   SQUARES & DRIZZLE WITH OLIVE OIL.

3. FOLD THE FOIL INTO A POUCH.
   BAKE AT 450°F (230°C) UNTIL
   TENDER, ABOUT 1 HOUR. THE
   BEETS MAY FINISH AT DIFFERENT
   TIMES, SO MAKE SURE TO CHECK
   BEFORE PULLING THEM OUT—
   REMOVE WHEN THEY CAN EASILY
   BE PIERCED WITH A KNIFE.

4. LET THE BEETS COOL OR SUBMERGE
   IN AN ICE BATH TO SPEED UP THE PROCESS.

5. CUT OFF THE STEM AND RUB THE SKIN
   OFF WITH YOUR THUMBS. USE A KNIFE
   FOR THE STUBBORN SPOTS.

Beet & Fennel Salad

SERVES 4

This salad has a great blend of textures and flavors. The deep sweetness of the roasted beets pairs nicely with the bright anise flavor of the fennel. The fennel also adds a great crunch. The salty feta cheese brings richness, and the lemon juice adds just the right amount of acidity.

---

2 CUPS (300 G) SLICED ROASTED BEETS
   (SEE PAGE 75 AND NOTE BELOW)

I CUP (85 G) THINLY SLICED FENNEL (ABOUT I BULB)

I PACKED TABLESPOON MINCED FRESH BASIL PLUS WHOLE
   LEAVES FOR GARNISH

I TABLESPOON OLIVE OIL

3 TABLESPOONS LEMON JUICE

1/2 CUP (60 G) CRUMBLED FETA CHEESE

SALT AND FRESHLY GROUND BLACK PEPPER TO TASTE

Gently toss the beets, fennel, minced basil, oil, and lemon juice together in a large bowl. Sprinkle with the cheese, season with salt and pepper, and garnish with a few basil leaves. Chill for I hour, then serve the salad cold.

NOTE:

Try to use Golden, Chiogga, or other non-red varieties of beets. You'll need 4-5 medium beets. Red beets will work perfectly fine; you'll just end up with a bright pink salad.

SLICE BEETS.

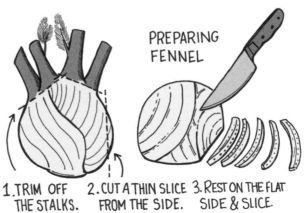

PREPARING FENNEL

1. TRIM OFF THE STALKS.   2. CUT A THIN SLICE FROM THE SIDE.   3. REST ON THE FLAT SIDE & SLICE.

ZUCCHINI

HOW TO GROW ZUCCHINI

Zucchini is a variety of summer squash, all of which can be used interchangeably in most recipes. Other varieties include squat, round pattypan squash, yellow crookneck squash, Lebanese squash, and yellow straight-neck squash. Summer squash are vigorous, fast-growing plants that will provide you with lots of fruit.

They thrive when directly sown in a sunny location, in a bed prepared with a thick layer of compost. Summer squash are large plants and need plenty of space, so allow 3 to 4 feet (.9 to 1.2 m) between plants. Luckily, you only need a few plants per family; otherwise you'll have more zucchini than you can handle. The best way to water these plants is by burying a soaker hose in the mulch around the plant. This prevents the leaves from getting wet, which could lead to powdery mildew. Light mulching around the plants is recommended, but the large leaves will keep weeds suppressed for the most part. When the plant has produced fruit, harvest it by using a sharp knife to cut them off the plant. You can harvest the baby zucchini or wait until they're about 6 inches (15 cm) long. Don't let them get too big, or the seeds will begin to harden and the flesh will be pithy. Regular harvesting will keep the fruit from growing too large.

CUT SQUASH OFF THE VINE

2 TO 3 IN. (5 TO 7.5 CM.)

ZUCCHINI   COUSA   PATTYPAN SQUASH   CROOKNECK SQUASH   YELLOW SQUASH

SERVES 4 TO 6

This galette is bursting at the seams with the freshness of summer. The flaky, nutty pastry contains fresh corn kernels, sweet pan-roasted tomatoes, and tender zucchini. Enjoy this on the patio with a chilled glass of rosé.

FOR THE FILLING

I TABLESPOON OLIVE OIL

I SMALL ONION, DICED

I ^{1}/2 CUPS (224 G) CHERRY TOMATOES

I CUP (125 G) DICED ZUCCHINI OR OTHER SUMMER SQUASH

I CUP (165 G) FRESH CORN KERNELS (FROM I EAR)

FOR THE CRUST

^{3}/4 CUP (90 G) ALL-PURPOSE FLOUR

^{1}/2 CUP (55 G) OAT FLOUR

^{1}/2 CUP (55 G) WHOLE-WHEAT FLOUR

^{1}/2 TEASPOON SALT

^{1}/2 CUP (I STICK/115 G) COLD UNSALTED BUTTER

ABOUT ^{1}/2 CUP (120 ML) ICE-COLD WATER

TO ASSEMBLE

^{1}/2 CUP (110 G) GOAT CHEESE

I EGG YOLK

Preheat the oven to 400°F (205°C). Make the filling: Heat the oil in a medium pan over medium-high heat. Add the onion and sauté until it starts to brown, about 3 minutes. Add the tomatoes and cook until they begin to burst, 10 to 13 minutes. Add the squash and cook for 3 minutes, then add the corn and cook for I minute more. Set aside.

[CONT.]

Make the crust: Sift together the flours and stir in the salt. Cut the butter into small pieces and rub it into the flour until the mixture resembles coarse meal. (This can be done by hand or in a food processor.) Slowly stir in up to ½ cup (120 ml) ice water, until the dough comes together. Roll out the dough on a floured surface until dough is about ¼ inch (6 mm) thick and 14 inches (35.5 cm) in diameter.

DOUGH ROLLED OUT 14 IN.

½ OF THE GOAT CHEESE.

Gently transfer the round to a parchment-lined baking sheet, or to a baking stone. Spread half the goat cheese in the center of the dough, leaving about 4 inches (10 cm) of dough around the perimeter. Pour the vegetable mixture on top of the cheese and dot with the remaining cheese. Fold the edges of the dough over the vegetables a little at the time, pinching the dough together to form pleats. The dough should cover the outer vegetables, leaving the center exposed. Whisk the egg yolk with 1 teaspoon water. Brush the outside of the pastry with the egg wash.

Bake for 30 to 40 minutes, until the crust is golden and the cheese has softened. Let cool slightly before cutting. Serve hot, warm, or at room temperature.

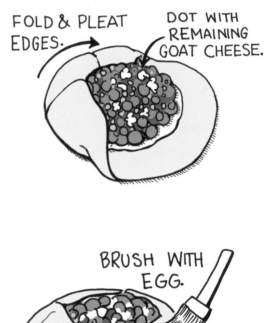

FOLD & PLEAT EDGES.

DOT WITH REMAINING GOAT CHEESE.

BRUSH WITH EGG.

CORN

Corn grows best in areas with a long frost-free growing season. Sow corn directly into the ground in holes 1 inch (2.5 cm) deep about 2 inches (5 cm) apart after all threat of frost has past and the soil temperature is over 60°F (16°C). Corn should be planted in blocks rather than rows to ensure better pollination. Once the kernels have sprouted, thin to every 15 inches (38 cm) by snipping the young plants at soil level.

Corn needs lots of nitrogen, so if the leaves on the corn start to turn a light yellow, you should use a nitrogen supplement. Water your corn evenly, especially when it develops its pollen tassel. Water

RIPE EARS

← THE SILKS ARE BROWN ¿ DRY.

← THE HUSK IS PLUMP.

↗ PEEL BACK THE HUSK TO EXPOSE A FEW KERNELS. POKE ONE TO SEE IF IT OOZES MILKY WHITE SAP.

stress will cause ears to grow with missing kernels. Begin checking the ears of corn about 3 weeks after the silk appears. Gently peel back the husk and pry off a kernel; if it's juicy, the ear is ripe. Most of the ears on the same stalk will ripen within a few days of each other. Use the corn or freeze the kernels the same day to prevent its sugars from turning to starch.

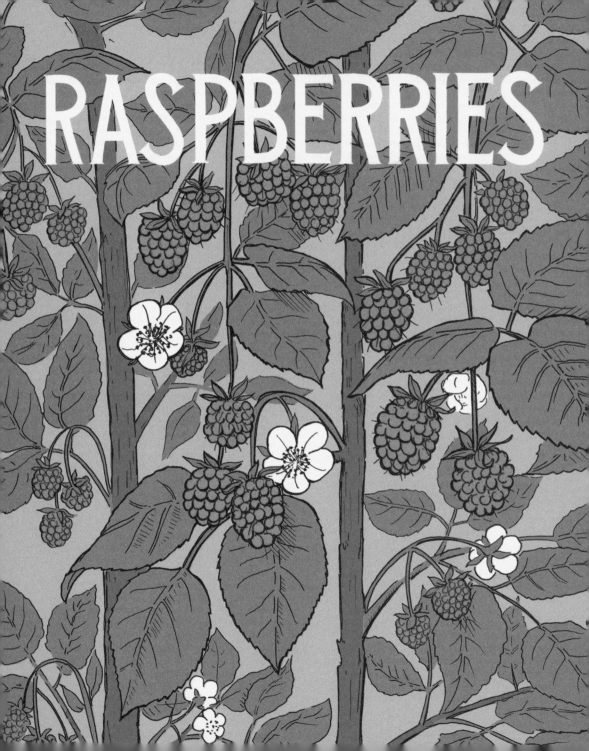

RASPBERRIES

HOW TO GROW RASPBERRIES

Raspberries grow on tall shrubs with cane-like stems that live for 2 years. There are two main kinds of raspberries: summer-bearing and everbearing. Summer-bearing canes fruit on their second summer, and new canes grow up to replace the canes that have fruited. Everbearing canes have a small second crop of fall berries that fruit on first-year canes. The following summer, there will be another larger crop on the same cane.

2ND-YEAR CANE (FLORICANE), PRUNE BACK AFTER SUMMER HARVEST.

1ST-YEAR CANE (PRIMOCANE), FALL CROP WILL GROW ON EVER-BEARERS.

For both types, prune back the second-year cane after harvesting.

Raspberries grow well in zones 3 to 9, but you should consult a horticulturist to choose a cultivar that is best suited for your climate. You can propagate raspberries from seed, but the easiest way to start your crop is by purchasing one-year-old plants. Plant these canes in a sunny location that isn't windy, about 2 feet (61 cm) apart, in rows 5 feet (1.5 m) apart.

As the plants grow, new canes will fill in the spaces. When harvesting the berries, use two hands and handle them with care. Don't drop the berries into a bucket. Raspberries don't ripen off the vine, so only pick when they're fully ripe. Eat or freeze them immediately.

HARVEST BERRIES WITH TWO HANDS.

SERVES 4

My favorite chocolate mousse recipe is by Elizabeth David, and I definitely had that in mind when creating this raspberry-flavored version. This is a grown-up dessert that's not for the faint of heart or only-milk-chocolate-loving wimps.

---

4 OUNCES (II5 G) DARK CHOCOLATE, AT LEAST 65% (I PREFER
   TCHO CHOCOLATE), PLUS MORE FOR GARNISH

1/4 CUP (60 ML) RUM, STRONG BREWED BLACK COFFEE,
   OR PLAIN WATER

4 EGGS, SEPARATED (SEE NOTE, PAGE 88)

2 CUPS (335 G) RASPBERRIES

WHIPPED CREAM (PAGE 54) FOR TOPPING

Put the chocolate and rum in the top of a double boiler over low heat. Stir continually until the chocolate is smooth and almost melted. Remove from the heat when it's almost completely melted, and keep stirring to finish melting the last bit. Don't overheat: This will cause the chocolate to seize and result in an undesirably clumpy mousse. Set aside to cool slightly, about 5 minutes.

Beat the egg yolks in a mixing bowl until smooth. Stir the chocolate into the egg yolks a spoonful at a time to slowly incorporate. In a separate bowl, whisk the egg whites until stiff peaks form. (This is most easily and effectively accomplished with an electric mixer, but with some perseverance, and maybe with the help of friend, you can whip up the whites by hand.)

[CONT.]

STIR CONSTANTLY.

KEEP HEAT ←LOW.

WHISK WHITES UNTIL PEAKS FORM.

Thoroughly fold the egg whites into the chocolate mixture, until completely blended. Spoon about 3 tablespoons of the mousse into a ramekin or pretty glass. Layer ¼ cup (40 g) raspberries on top, then spoon on a few more tablespoons mousse. Top with ¼ cup (42 g) raspberries. Repeat to make three more servings. Cover and refrigerate for at least 30 minutes, up to 3 hours, before serving. Just before serving, top with a healthy dollop of whipped cream and shave a little chocolate over the cream for garnish.

NOTE:

This recipe contains raw egg, so be mindful of dietary restrictions.

FOLD IN WHITES UNTIL BLENDED.

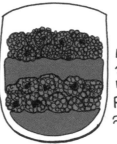

LAYER:
1/4 CUP RASPBERRIES
≈ 3 TBS. MOUSSE
1/4 CUP RASPBERRIES
≈ 3 TBS. MOUSSE

BELL PEPPERS

Bell peppers thrive in warm weather
and do well when started indoors 8
weeks before the last frost. Peppers
have a delicate root system, so use peat
pots that can be planted directly into
the ground; they also do well in large
containers. Sow seeds three per pot, and
put them in a warm sunny place. Once
the soil outside is over 60°F (16°C),
begin hardening off your plants (see
page 19). Peppers are sensitive little
plants and need to be gently eased into
their new environment or they'll go into
shock. Water 1 to 2 inches (2.5 to 5 cm)
per week. Harvest the peppers by cutting
them off the plant, not by pulling them.

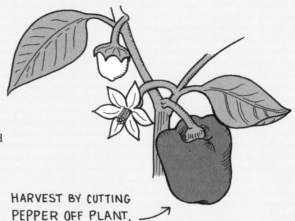

HARVEST BY CUTTING
PEPPER OFF PLANT.

FENNEL

The fennel bulb that we eat is actually an
enlarged stem at the base of the plant,
and the best cultivar for this purpose
is the Florence variety. The seeds
can be sown directly into the dirt and
gently raked in. Fennel also grows well
in containers. As the plant begins to
sprout, make sure to pile dirt around its
base to blanch the bulb (this keeps the
bulb from turning green.) The bulb is
ready to harvest when it measures 3 to 4
inches (7.5 to 10 cm) across. To harvest,
cut the entire plant, level to the ground.
If you're careful not to damage the
roots, another bulb may grow up from
the same plant.

← MOUND MULCH
OVER THE BULB
TO BLANCH.

EQUAL DAY & NIGHT

At the start of fall, the sun gets lower in the sky, and you can feel things beginning to slow down. Where I live, we get a few weeks of temperate weather before the rains set in, and I try to enjoy the lingering warmth and light as much as possible. Even though the days are getting shorter and cooler, there is still plenty of freshness to be enjoyed from the garden. Fall produce is earthier and more savory than the bursting freshness of spring and summer; delicate peas and berries make way for root vegetables and hard squash. The recipes for fall reflect the hardiness and earthy sweetness of this produce. The flavors are deeper and more complex, and the dishes are a little richer.

As life moves back inside, it is easier to find time to prepare for the colder seasons. Toward the end of the fall, I like to preserve the remaining bounty of my summer garden by canning some tomatoes and making preserves (see page 158).

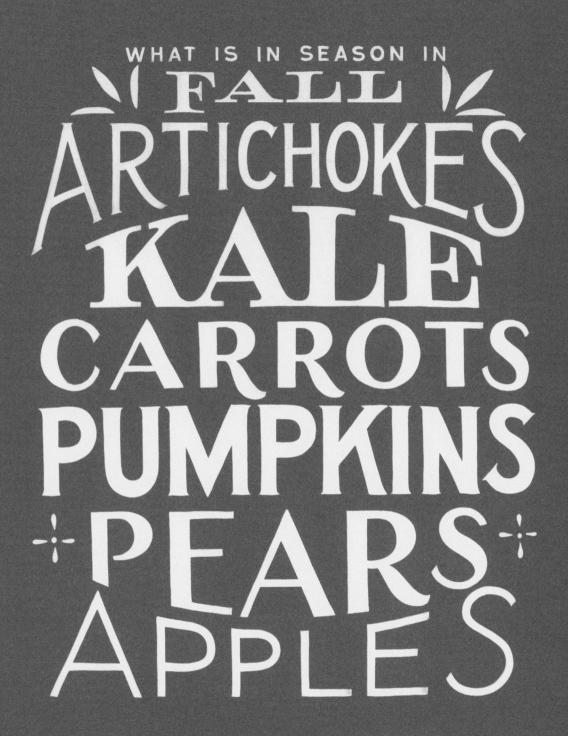

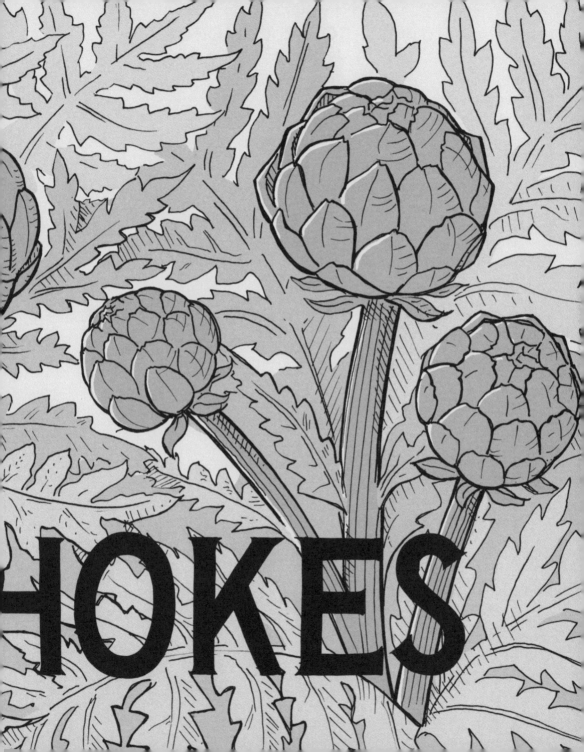

HOW TO GROW ARTICHOKES

Artichokes are a large perennial plant related to the thistle. The artichoke grows best in zones 7 or higher, where they survive the mild, relatively frost-free winters. In areas with colder winters, the plants can be grown as annuals, rather than perennials, as long as there are 100 consecutive frost-free days.

There are multiple ways to start artichokes in your garden. You can start them from seed, you can plant the dormant roots of a mature plant, or you can get a split from someone with a mature plant. Plant them in full sun, spacing the plants 3 to 4 feet (.9 to 1.2 m) apart.

Perennial artichoke plants will produce for five years. Artichokes are heavy feeders: They need rich soil supplemented with a side dressing of compost or chicken manure on a monthly basis. The edible part of the artichoke is actually the immature flower bud, and the plants will produce flowers in spring and again in the fall. Harvest the buds when they're hefty but still tightly closed by cutting them from the stalk with a serrated knife about 2 inches (5 cm) below the bud. Once they blossom, they're no longer edible, but they are an attractive flower.

ARTICHOKE BLOSSOM
(PRETTY, BUT NOT
GOOD TO EAT)

HARVEST WHEN

STILL TIGHTLY CLOSED

USE A SHARP KNIFE TO CUT OFF THE BUD.

LEAVE A FEW INCHES OF STEM.

ANATOMY OF AN ARTICHOKE

THORN

TENDER INNER LEAVES

TOUGH OUTER LEAVES

CHOKE

HEART

EDIBLE PART OF LEAF

STEM

EAT THE LEAVES FROM THE OUTSIDE IN:

SCRAPE THE SMALL AMOUNT OF MEAT OFF WITH YOUR TEETH...

THEN DISCARD THE TOUGH PART OF THE LEAF.

SCOOP OUT & DISCARD THE CHOKE.

SINK YOUR TEETH INTO THE HEART & ENJOY.

Roasted Artichokes with Aioli

SERVES 4

Before moving to California, the only artichokes I'd had were the canned hearts. Out here, though, fresh artichokes are ubiquitous, and I learned how to properly prepare and eat them. Artichokes are widely available at farmers' markets outside of California, so if you're not familiar with the vegetable don't let the spiny exterior deter you. You're in for a treat.

FOR THE ARTICHOKES

4 ARTICHOKES

8 TO 12 CLOVES GARLIC, WHOLE

2 WHOLE LEMONS

4 TABLESPOONS (60 ML) OLIVE OIL

PINCH OF SALT

FOR THE LEMON AIOLI

1 CLOVE GARLIC, FINELY MINCED

SALT

1 EGG YOLK, AT ROOM TEMPERATURE

4 TABLESPOONS (60 ML) MILD-FLAVORED OLIVE OIL

2 TABLESPOONS LEMON JUICE

FRESHLY GROUND BLACK PEPPER

Make the artichokes: Preheat the oven to 425°F (220°C). With a sharp knife, cut off the stem and the top 1 to 1 ½ inches (2.5 to 4 cm) of an artichoke. Slice a lemon in half and rub the cut parts of the artichoke with the lemon. Use your fingers to separate and spread the leaves of the artichoke apart, to loosen the layers. Use a knife to pierce through the center of the artichoke. Insert a few cloves of garlic into the center and between the leaves. Put the artichoke in a bowl and squeeze the juice of ½ lemon and 1 tablespoon of the oil over the top.

[CONT.]

SLICE THE TOP & STEM OFF. RUB WITH LEMON.

Sprinkle with a pinch of salt. Tear off a
sheet of heavy-duty aluminum foil and
place the artichoke in the middle facing
up. Pour the juice and oil from the bowl
over the top of the artichoke, and wrap the
foil around it tightly to make a semi-air-
tight seal. Repeat with a second sheet of
foil. Repeat this process with the remaining artichokes, lemon juice, and olive
oil and place them all in a baking dish.
Bake for 1 hour 15 minutes for medium
artichokes; the baking time will be slightly
longer for larger artichokes and shorter
for smaller ones. They're done when the
center can easily be pierced with a knife.

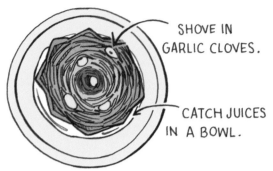

SHOVE IN
GARLIC CLOVES.

CATCH JUICES
IN A BOWL.

Make the aioli: While the artichokes are
cooking, sprinkle the minced garlic with salt
and set it aside. Thoroughly whisk the egg yolk
until it's smooth. Slowly start adding the oil a
drop or two at a time while whisking continuously. Once you've incorporated about half
the oil, you can begin adding a little more
with each pour. (Slowly adding the oil emulsifies
the oil and yolk; rushing this process will cause the
mixture to separate.) Once the oil is completely
incorporated, you should have a thick, yellow
mixture. Whisk in the lemon juice a little at time,
until incorporated. Stir in the garlic, and season
with salt and pepper to taste. Remove the
artichokes from the oven and let them rest until
they are cool enough to handle. Unwrap and serve
with a bowl of the aioli for dipping. Be sure to have
an extra bowl on hand for discarded leaves.

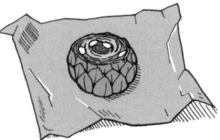

USE HEAVY-DUTY ALUMINUM FOIL.

WHISK
CONTINUOUSLY.

HOW TO GROW KALE

Kale is a hardy green that grows best in cool weather. It thrives in areas that have mild winters. Although the leaves taste sweeter when they've been kissed with frost, these plants prefer temperatures to remain above 15°F (-9°C). Sow seeds ½ inch (12 mm) deep in rows 2 feet (61 cm) apart. When the seedlings are a few inches (or centimeters) high, thin them to 12 inches (30.5 cm) apart. Don't toss these baby greens, though: They're tender and delicious in salad or quickly sautéed in butter.

Once your plants are mature, harvest the leaves when they're about the size of your hand by picking just a few off of each plant, starting on the outside. Make sure not to cut off the terminal bud at the top, center of the plant, as this is where new growth originates. Your kale plants will continuously produce new leaves through their growing season as long as the terminal bud remains intact.

THIN

THIN

THIN

1 PLANT EVERY 12 IN.

HARVEST
KALE LEAVES
FROM THE
OUTSIDE IN.

VARIETIES OF KALE

DINOSAUR/
LACINATO/
NERO KALE

CURLY
KALE

RED
RUSSIAN
KALE

SERVES 4 AS A MAIN DISH, OR 6 TO 8 AS A SIDE

This salad can be made several hours ahead of time and can be kept covered in the refrigerator until you're ready to serve it. In fact, I think it's even slightly better after sitting. If the leaves wilt slightly, it makes for easier chewing. The tough kale leaves stand up to being predressed, and the lemon juice in the dressing keeps the apples from turning brown.

CUT OUT TOUGH CENTER STALK.

ROLL UP & CHOP.

DICE APPLES.

SQUEEZE.

2 BUNCHES DINOSAUR KALE (ALSO KNOWN AS NERO OR LACINATO KALE)

1/2 CUP (60 G) FINELY GRATED PECORINO CHEESE

1/4 CUP (60 ML) CRÈME FRAÎCHE (SEE PAGE 38)

3 TABLESPOONS LEMON JUICE

1/3 CUP (75 ML) OLIVE OIL

SALT AND FRESHLY GROUND BLACK PEPPER

2 CRISP, SWEET APPLES SUCH AS PINK LADY OR HONEYCRISP, DICED

1/2 CUP (50 G) FINELY CHOPPED WALNUTS

Tear or cut the tough center stalk from each kale leaf and discard it. Chop the leaves into bite-size pieces and put them in a large serving bowl. In a separate bowl, combine the cheese, crème fraîche, and lemon juice. Slowly whisk in the oil, adding a little at a time. Add a dash of salt and pepper to taste. Add the apples and walnuts to the kale. Pour the dressing over the salad. With clean hands, toss the salad and massage the dressing into the kale. Really work it in by squeezing the leaves and mashing them together (massaging the kale breaks down some of the tough fibers of the leaves). Season with more salt and freshly ground pepper if needed. Serve, or refrigerate and serve up to several hours later.

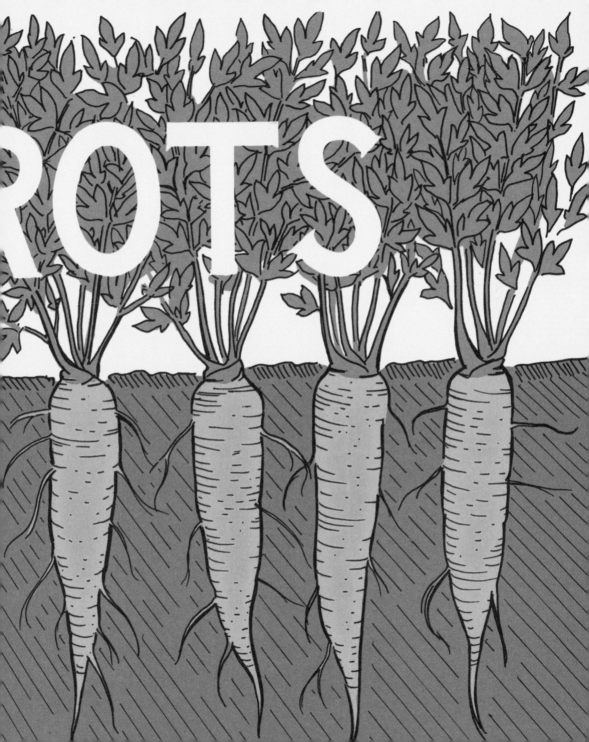

HOW TO GROW CARROTS

Carrots are a cool-weather vegetable that can be sown directly into the ground 3 weeks before the last expected frost for a spring harvest and 2 to 3 months before the first expected frost for a fall harvest. Carrots need to be planted in at least 12 inches (30.5 cm) of loose soil for their long tap roots to have room to grow. Either double dig your garden by digging through the topsoil and subsoil and raking out roots and stones to loosen the soil, or plant in a deep raised bed.

When you're ready to plant, dig a shallow trench for your row, evenly sprinkle in the carrot seeds, and loosely cover with ½ inch (12 mm) of soil. Begin the next row 12 inches (30.5 cm) away from the first. Keep the soil evenly moist during germination, without flooding and washing away the seeds. You should see the carrots emerge after 1 to 3 weeks. When the carrot tops are a few inches or centimeters high, thin so there's one every 3 to 4 inches (7.5 to 10 cm), snipping the plants at soil level instead of pulling them up. Keep the plants evenly moist as they're growing. Carrots mature in about 2½ months. The fall crop can be covered with a thick layer of mulch and left in the ground until needed. If they're left in the ground into the spring, carrots will flower and produce seeds in their second year.

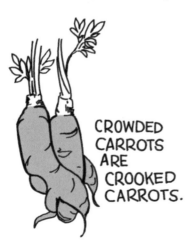

CROWDED CARROTS ARE CROOKED CARROTS.

SERVES 4 TO 6

This soup is full-bodied, and has a nice balance of flavor between the curry spices and the sweetness of the carrots and honey. Most of the ingredients are pantry staples, and the prep time is fairly quick, making this a great soup for a weeknight meal.

8 CARROTS

3 TABLESPOONS UNSALTED BUTTER

I YELLOW ONION, DICED

I TABLESPOON MINCED FRESH GINGER

I TABLESPOON CURRY POWDER

^{1}/2 CUP (120 ML) HEAVY CREAM

4 CUPS (960 ML) VEGETABLE BROTH

I TABLESPOON HONEY

I TEASPOON SALT

PEEL &
ROUGHLY CHOP.

Wash, peel, and roughly chop the carrots. In a large pot over medium heat, lightly brown the butter. Add the onion and ginger and cook, stirring frequently, until fragrant, about 3 minutes. Add the carrots and sauté for 10 minutes, and then add the curry powder and cook for 1 more minute. Pour in the cream, stirring and scraping the bottom of the pot to deglaze it. Cover the pot and cook for 5 minutes, checking every so often to make sure it doesn't get dry. Add the broth, bring to a simmer, and cook until the carrots are very tender, 10 to 15 minutes more. Using an immersion blender (or an upright blender, in batches), puree the soup until it's completely smooth. Stir in the honey and salt and serve warm.

DEGLAZE THE
BOTTOM OF THE POT.

PUREE UNTIL SMOOTH.

PUMPKINS

HOW TO GROW PUMPKINS

Pumpkins are a hard squash that require a long growing period and a lot of space. They are sensitive plants: They need plenty of moisture, light, and warm soil. If you live in a cooler climate, start them indoors in a peat pot that can be planted directly into the ground. The soil temperature should be 60° to 65°F (16° to 18°C) before the pumpkins are planted in the garden.

Pumpkins are heavy feeders, so make sure to add plenty of compost to the soil before planting your seedlings in your garden. If you're planting a vine variety, allow for at least 50 square feet (5 m²) per plant. You can train the vines in one direction if you don't have space for them to sprawl. Your pumpkin has reached maturity when it's no longer getting larger (the time it takes varies among the different cultivars). You can check this by thumping it with your hand. If it makes a deep hollow sound, it's ready. Use a sharp knife to cut the pumpkin from the vine, leaving several inches of stem. Pick it up by the bottom (not the stem) and set it in the sunshine for a week to cure the skin, then store it in a cool, dry place until you're ready to cook (or decorate) with it.

VINES NEED ROOM TO ROAM

CURE IN THE SUNSHINE

SERVES 4

These little pumpkin quiches are my signature Thanksgiving dish (but they make a great dinner throughout the fall). It's not often that you get to enjoy the unadulterated taste of the pumpkin, and it's a real treat. You eat these mini-quiches by scooping out a little of the pumpkin and a little of the custard in each spoonful. As an added bonus, the pumpkin halves look absolutely lovely on the table.

2 (1-POUND/455-G) SUGAR (OR PIE) PUMPKINS

2 TABLESPOONS UNSALTED BUTTER

2 YELLOW ONIONS, DICED

SALT

1/2 CUP (120 ML) HEAVY CREAM

2 EGGS, AT ROOM TEMPERATURE

FRESHLY GROUND BLACK PEPPER

1 TABLESPOON OLIVE OIL

4 TABLESPOONS (30 G) GRATED PARMESAN CHEESE

ABOUT 1/2 BAGUETTE, CUT INTO 1-INCH (2.5-CM) CUBES

Preheat the oven to 350°F (175°C). Slice the stem off each pumpkin without cutting off too much of the flesh. Make sure you don't cut into the hollow of the pumpkin; you'll need it to hold your custard. Cut each pumpkin into equal halves around its equator and scrape out the seeds and fibers. Place the pumpkin halves, cut side down, in a baking dish that is large enough to accommodate them, and pour about ¼ inch (6 mm) of water in the bottom of the dish. Bake the pumpkins for 15 to 20 minutes, depending on the size of your pumpkins. Pumpkins larger than 1 pound (455 g) will need a little more time. When you have removed the pumpkins from the oven, turn up the oven temperature to 375°F (190°C).

SHALLOWLY SLICE OFF THE STEM.

SLICE IN HALF.

[CONT.]

While the pumpkins are baking, melt the butter in a wide, heavy-bottomed sauté pan over medium heat. Add the onions and sauté them for a few minutes. Add a pinch of salt (to help the onions release water) and continue cooking for about 20 minutes, or until the onions caramelize. They are done when they're a deep brown and have significantly reduced in volume. Scrape them into a bowl and set aside.

In the same pan used to cook the onion, gently warm the cream to remove the chill. In a separate bowl, whisk together the warm cream and the eggs. Season with a few dashes of salt and pepper. Turn the pumpkins cut side up and place them on a baking sheet large enough for each to sit flat. Brush the exposed rim of each half with oil. Put 3 or 4 cubes of bread in the bottom of each pumpkin half. Divide the caramelized onions evenly among the pumpkin halves. Pour the egg mixture over the bread and the onions to cover (without filling them to the brim). Sprinkle 1 tablespoon cheese over each half. Bake for 30 minutes. Serve warm.

NOTE:

To increase the number of servings, add 1 onion, 1 tablespoon butter, ¼ cup cream, 1 egg, and 2 tablespoons Parmesan cheese per extra pumpkin (2 servings).

¼ INCH WATER.

STEAM PUMPKINS UPSIDE DOWN IN THE OVEN.

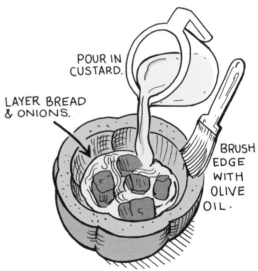

POUR IN CUSTARD.

LAYER BREAD & ONIONS.

BRUSH EDGE WITH OLIVE OIL.

HOW TO GROW PEARS

It's very important to choose a variety of pear for your garden that is suited to your region. If you live outside of the arid western regions of the United States, you'll have to contend with fire blight. However, choosing resistant varieties that suit where you live goes a long way toward preventing blight. Dwarf varieties that stay under 20 feet (6 m) are ideal for ease of harvesting and conserving space. To get your pears started, purchase year-old "whips" of two different varieties from a horticulturist and plant them 15 feet (4.5 m) apart in your garden. You need to plant at least two different varieties of pears, because they need to cross-pollinate to bear fruit. Dwarf varieties will fruit in 3 to 5 years. Harvest pears when the lenticels (the little flecks on the skin of the pear) turn from a light tan color to brown—the pear should still be hard. Ripen pears off the tree at room temperature.

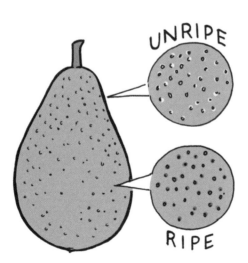

UNRIPE

RIPE

I-YEAR-OLD WHIPS

PLANT AT LEAST
TWO VARIETIES FOR
CROSS POLLINATION.

HOW TO PEEL AND SLICE PEARS

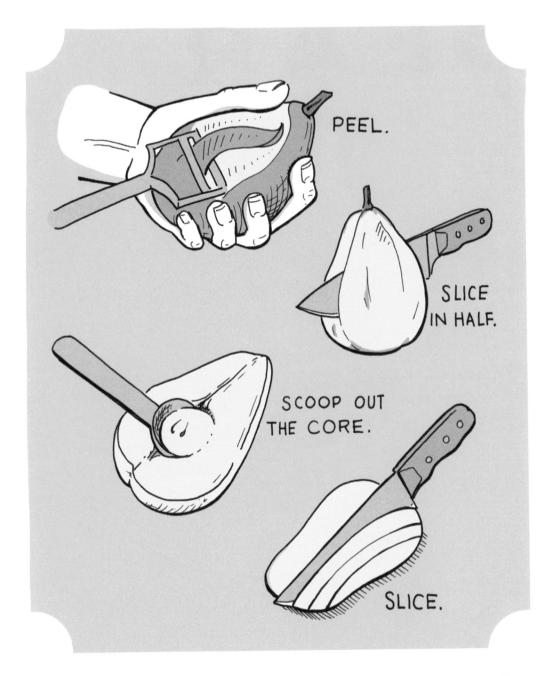

PEEL.

SLICE IN HALF.

SCOOP OUT THE CORE.

SLICE.

SERVES 6 TO 8

I love freeform tarts. They're beautiful, rustic, and super easy to put together. I added a little whole-wheat pastry flour to make a heartier, slightly nutty-tasting crust. The pears in this recipe could easily be replaced with apples or a mixture of pears and apples, if you prefer.

FOR THE CRUST

1/2 CUP (55 G) PLUS 2 TABLESPOONS ALL-PURPOSE FLOUR

1/2 CUP (60 G) WHOLE-WHEAT PASTRY FLOUR

1/2 TEASPOON SALT

1 TABLESPOON GRANULATED SUGAR

1/2 CUP (1 STICK/115 G) UNSALTED BUTTER

2 TO 3 TABLESPOONS ICE-COLD WATER

FOR THE FILLING

2 POUNDS (910 G) PEARS, PEELED, CORED, AND THINLY SLICED
    (ABOUT 4 CUPS) (SEE PAGE 119)

1 TABLESPOON LEMON JUICE

1/4 CUP (50 G) GRANULATED SUGAR

1 TABLESPOON CORNSTARCH

1/2 TEASPOON GROUND CINNAMON

1 TABLESPOON UNSALTED BUTTER

TO ASSEMBLE

1 EGG, BEATEN

1 TABLESPOON COARSE TURBINADO SUGAR

Make the crust: Combine the flours, salt, and granulated sugar in the bowl of a food processor. Pulse two or three times to combine. Cut the butter into small pieces and add it to the bowl of the food processor. Process until the mixture resembles coarse sand. (If you don't have a food processor, you can work the butter into the flour

[CONT.]

by rubbing it in between your fingers.) Add a few tablespoons of ice water to the mixture and pulse a few times (or mix with a wooden spoon) until the dough begins to come together.

Empty the dough onto a clean work surface and form it into a ball, trying not to work it more than necessary. If the dough is too crumbly and not staying together, add 1 tablespoon of ice water at a time until it reaches the right consistency. Wrap the dough in plastic and flatten it into a disk. Refrigerate for about 1 hour. You can make the dough a day ahead of time.

Make the filling: Slice the pears, and toss them in the lemon juice in a large bowl. Then add the granulated sugar, cornstarch, and cinnamon and toss to evenly coat. Set aside. Remove the dough from the refrigerator and preheat the oven to 400°F (205°C). Line a rimmed baking sheet with parchment paper. On a floured surface, roll the dough out to a 13-inch (33-cm) round, just under ¼ inch (6 mm) thick. Transfer the round to the prepared baking sheet. Mound the pear mixture in the center of the crust, leaving 3 to 4 inches (7.5 to 10 cm) of dough around the edges. Cut the butter into small pieces and distribute them over the top. Fold the edges of the dough over the fruit a little at a time, pinching the dough together to form pleats. The dough should cover the outer fruit, leaving the center exposed. Don't worry about making it perfect, but make sure there are no cracks. It just has to hold the fruit and the juices in. Brush the exposed dough with the beaten egg and sprinkle the turbinado sugar over the dough and the fruit. Bake for 30 to 35 minutes, until golden and bubbly. Serve warm or at room temperature.

THINLY SLICE.

TOSS PEARS IN
LEMON JUICE.

MOUND PEAR MIXTURE IN
THE CENTER OF THE CRUST.

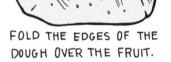

FOLD THE EDGES OF THE
DOUGH OVER THE FRUIT.

APPLES

To start your apple orchard, buy dormant 1-year-old plants with healthy
roots from your nursery. Consult with a
horticulturist to choose disease-resistant
varieties that are suited to your region.
You can choose to plant either dwarf,
semi-dwarf, or standard-size trees,
depending on how much space you have.
Dwarf and semi-dwarf trees bear fruit
in 3 to 4 years, while standard trees fruit
after 5 to 8 years. Most apple trees can-
not self pollinate or pollinate another
tree of the same variety, so you will need
to plant two different varieties of apples
so the bees can pollinate the flowers.
Choose a sunny location for your trees
that is evenly moist. If you're planting a
dwarf variety, it will need the support of
a fence or stake because the weight of the
fruit can uproot the tree.

STAKE DWARF TREES

The winter months are characterized by stillness. As the short days and cold weather push us back indoors, everyone—and everything—quiets down. Honeybees stop working and instead huddle around their queen to keep her warm; chickens slow their laying. Depending on where you live, your garden may also slow down considerably, if not come to a complete halt. Although mild climates can continue to support some cool-season crops like brussels sprouts (see page 134), and citrus is ripening in the warmer areas, gardeners in most regions spend their late-winter months thinking about spring and starting some seedlings indoors.

The flavors of the winter are rich and savory. The hard root vegetables that are prevalent in the winter months stand up well to being roasted, so I do a lot of baking and roasting in the winter (also an excuse to run the oven and warm the kitchen up). This is the time of year to break out your dried and canned goods and lean on your spices for added flavoring.

PARSNIPS

HOW TO GROW PARSNIPS

Parsnips are easy to grow, and are fairly disease resistant. They require a long growing period and should be planted early in the spring for a late fall or winter harvest. Double dig your soil 12 to 15 inches (30.5 to 38 cm) deep or plant in a raised bed, and mix in a few inches of compost for added nutrients.

PARSNIP SEED

MULCH DEEPLY.

Plant your seeds directly into the soil ½ inch (12 mm) deep and 1 inch (2.5 cm) apart. Your rows should be 6 inches (15 cm) apart. When the plants are 6 inches (15 cm) tall, thin to 3 to 6 inches (7.5 to 15 cm), snipping the seedlings off at soil level so that you don't damage the neighboring plants by pulling them up. Parsnips are mature in about 4 months but are sweetest after they've been exposed to frost. After a hard frost you can either harvest them right away or cover them with several inches of mulch and harvest them throughout the winter as needed.

TASTE BEST WHEN KISSED BY FROST. THEY CAN BE LEFT IN THE GROUND UNTIL NEEDED.

PARSNIP HUMMUS

with HOMEMADE CRACKERS

SERVES 8 AS AN APPETIZER

Traditional hummus is made with chickpeas and tahini, but replacing the chickpeas with parsnips adds a subtle sweetness that I really like. The homemade crackers are better than anything you've had out of a box, and you can customize the toppings to your taste. The whole-wheat flour makes the crackers taste a little nutty, and I like to break them into uneven pieces for rustic charm.

FOR THE CRACKERS

3/4 CUP (90 G) ALL-PURPOSE FLOUR, OR MORE IF NEEDED

3/4 CUP (90 G) WHOLE-WHEAT FLOUR

1/2 TEASPOON INSTANT YEAST

I TEASPOON SALT

2 TABLESPOONS OLIVE OIL

I TABLESPOON HONEY

1/2 CUP (120 ML) WARM WATER, OR MORE IF NEEDED

OPTIONAL TOPPINGS (SEE NOTE, PAGE 133)

FOR THE HUMMUS

I POUND (455 G) PARSNIPS, PEELED AND
  CHOPPED INTO I-INCH PIECES

1/4 CUP (60 ML) TAHINI

1/4 CUP (60 ML) OLIVE OIL

1/4 CUP (60 ML) LEMON JUICE (FROM
  ABOUT 2 LEMONS)

I CLOVE GARLIC

2 TEASPOONS GROUND CUMIN

SALT AND FRESHLY GROUND BLACK PEPPER

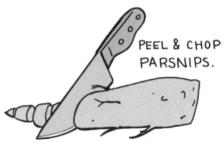

PEEL & CHOP
PARSNIPS.

Make the cracker dough: Combine the flours, yeast, and salt in a large bowl. Mix in the oil and honey. Stir in the warm water little by little until a ball of dough forms. Add more flour or water a little at a time until you achieve the right consistency. Turn the dough out

[CONT.]

onto a floured surface and knead it until it's smooth and pliable, about 5 minutes. Put the dough in a lightly oiled bowl and cover with plastic wrap. Let the dough sit in a warm place for 1 hour to 1 hour 30 minutes.

LET THE DOUGH REST.

Make the hummus: While the dough rests, put the parsnips in a large pot and cover with water. Over high heat, bring the water to a boil, then reduce the heat to medium and simmer the parsnips for about 20 minutes, until you can easily pierce them with a fork. Drain. In the bowl of a food processor, combine the parsnips, tahini, oil, lemon juice, garlic, and cumin and puree until smooth. Alternatively, you can return the parsnips to the pot you boiled them in, combine the ingredients, and use an immersion blender to puree. Season with salt and pepper to taste and set aside to cool.

COOKED PARSNIPS
TAHINI
OLIVE OIL
LEMON JUICE
GARLIC
CUMIN

To finish the crackers, Preheat the oven to 350°F (175°C). Put a baking stone in the oven to preheat, or use a half sheet pan lined with parchment paper. Turn the dough out onto a lightly floured surface and divide into two equal pieces. Return one half to the oiled bowl and cover. Roll the other half of the dough out to the approximate dimensions of your baking stone or baking sheet. It should be very thin, about $1/16$ inch (2 mm) thick or less. Transfer the dough to the preheated baking

stone or the prepared baking sheet. Add
toppings if desired and use your rolling pin
to gently press them into the dough. If you
want uniformly sized crackers, use a pizza
cutter to score your dough. Otherwise,
you can just break the cracker sheet into
freeform uneven pieces once it cools (my
preferred method). Bake the crackers for
18 minutes, turning the pan about halfway
through to evenly bake. When done, they'll
be brown on the edges and bubbly and wavy
throughout. Remove from the oven and let
cool on a wire rack. Repeat with the remaining half of the dough. Once cool, break apart
and serve with your hummus.

NOTE:
You can add toppings to your crackers if you
wish. Some of my favorites are: salt, fresh
cracked black pepper, cumin seeds, fennel
seeds, caraway seeds, poppy seeds, sesame
seeds, paprika, and dried rosemary. Pick
one or two or make "everything" crackers.
You can make the crackers a day in advance
if you're having a dinner party—after they've
completely cooled, store them in an airtight
container until you're ready to use them.

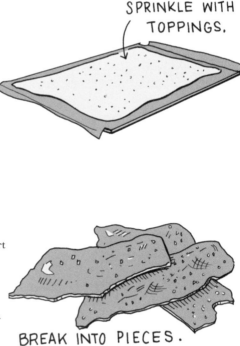

SPRINKLE WITH TOPPINGS.

BREAK INTO PIECES.

BRUSSELS
SPROUTS

HOW TO GROW BRUSSELS SPROUTS

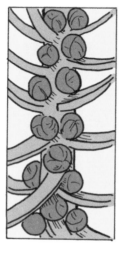

TWIST OFF THE STALK.

HARVEST FROM THE BOTTOM UP.

REMOVE DEAD, OR YELLOW, LEAVES.

Brussels sprouts need space, time, and a kiss of frost to taste their best. They take about 100 days to mature, so make sure you plant them 4 months before the first frost for a late fall through early winter harvest. Prepare your bed in an area that gets full sun, and mix in compost. Sow the seeds ½ inch (12 mm) deep and 3 inches (7.5 cm) apart, spacing rows 30 inches (75 cm) apart. When the seedlings are about 6 inches (15 cm) tall, thin to one plant every 24 inches (60 cm). As the plant matures, the sprouts will form on the trunk of the plant at the base of the leaves. Harvest the sprouts once they're about 1 inch (2.5 cm) wide by twisting them off the trunk, starting from the bottom and working your way up as they mature. Remove yellow, dead leaves as the sprouts mature to give the sprouts more room to grow. Although Brussels sprouts taste great after they've been touched by a light frost, make sure to harvest any remaining sprouts by cutting down the whole stalk before the first deep freeze.

24 IN. APART

ROWS 30 IN. APART

HOW TO CLEAN BRUSSELS SPROUTS

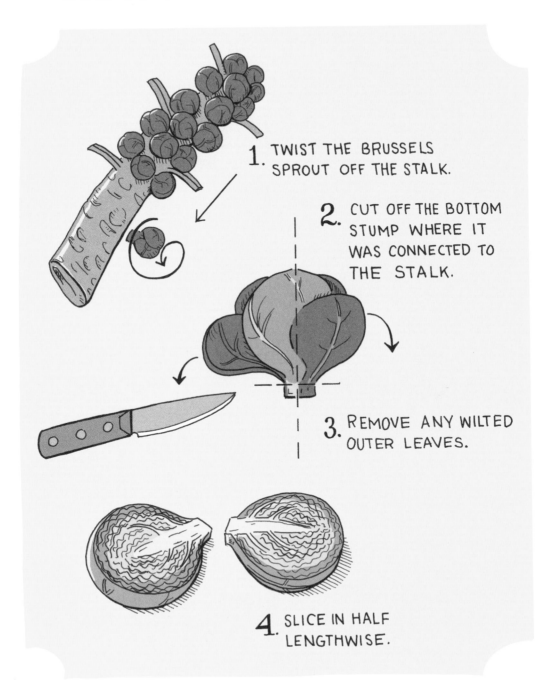

1. TWIST THE BRUSSELS SPROUT OFF THE STALK.

2. CUT OFF THE BOTTOM STUMP WHERE IT WAS CONNECTED TO THE STALK.

3. REMOVE ANY WILTED OUTER LEAVES.

4. SLICE IN HALF LENGTHWISE.

SERVES 4

This is a simple dish that offers a comforting blend of sweet and savory. The sweetness of the apples will win over anyone who might be a little skeptical about eating brussels sprouts.

---

1 POUND (455 G) BRUSSELS SPROUTS

3 SHALLOTS, THINLY SLICED LENGTHWISE

1 SWEET RED APPLE (SUCH AS HONEYCRISP), QUARTERED, CORED, AND THINLY SLICED

2 TABLESPOONS OLIVE OIL

1/4 TEASPOON SALT

1/4 TEASPOON FRESHLY GROUND BLACK PEPPER

JUICE OF 1 LEMON

THINLY SLICE LENGTHWISE.

Preheat the oven to 425°F (220°C). Clean the Brussels sprouts following the instructions on page 137. In a large bowl, toss the Brussels sprouts, shallots, and apple in the oil, salt, and pepper. Arrange in a single layer in a baking dish. Bake for 20 to 30 minutes, until caramelized. Squeeze the lemon juice over the Brussels sprouts and serve.

2 TBS. OLIVE OIL

BAKE UNTIL CARAMELIZED.

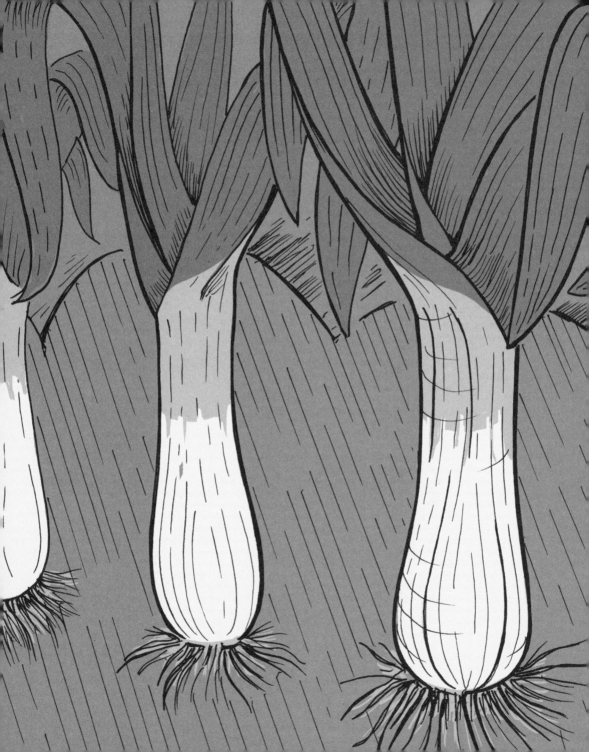

HOW TO GROW LEEKS

Leeks are a mild-flavored cousin to onions. They can be sown in the early spring for a late fall or early winter harvest. Like parsnips, they can be left in the ground until needed, but should be harvested before the ground fully freezes over.

Start seeds in flats. When the seedlings are about 10 inches (25 cm) tall, dig a trench 6 inches (15 cm) deep and plant them 3 to 4 inches (7.5 to 10 cm) apart. Leeks do well in deep containers and raised beds, as well as planted straight into the ground in soil that is moist (heavily mulched), well drained, and high in nitrogen. As the plants continue to grow, mound a few inches of dirt around the base of each plant to blanch the stalk; this keeps it from turning green and you'll have more of the tender white part.

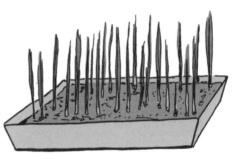

When they've reached scallion size, harvest every other plant. Once they've reached 1 inch (2.5 cm) or more in diameter, harvest the remaining leeks as needed.

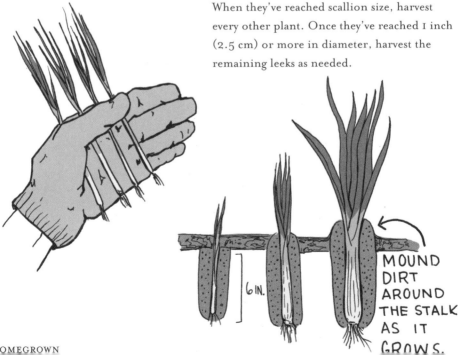

6 IN.

MOUND DIRT AROUND THE STALK AS IT GROWS.

HOW TO TRIM LEEKS

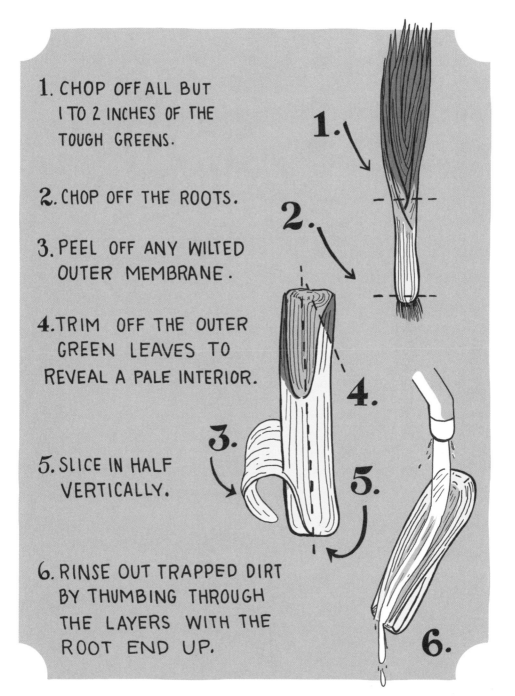

1. CHOP OFF ALL BUT 1 TO 2 INCHES OF THE TOUGH GREENS.

2. CHOP OFF THE ROOTS.

3. PEEL OFF ANY WILTED OUTER MEMBRANE.

4. TRIM OFF THE OUTER GREEN LEAVES TO REVEAL A PALE INTERIOR.

5. SLICE IN HALF VERTICALLY.

6. RINSE OUT TRAPPED DIRT BY THUMBING THROUGH THE LAYERS WITH THE ROOT END UP.

POTATO and LEEK SOUP

SERVES 4 TO 6

Potato and leek soup is a classic for a reason: It is smooth, velvety, and very satis-fying. It isn't overly fussy to prepare, and the smell of the leeks and garlic sautéing in butter is simply divine. This is a hearty soup that can stand alone as a meal or be served in a smaller portion as a starter.

---

2 TABLESPOONS UNSALTED BUTTER

3 CUPS (265 G) LEEKS, FINELY CHOPPED
   (PALE GREEN AND WHITE PARTS ONLY)

2 CLOVES GARLIC, MINCED

I ¹/2 TEASPOONS SALT

I ¹/2 POUNDS (680 G) RUSSET POTATOES,
   PEELED AND DICED (ABOUT 2 LARGE)

3 STALKS CELERY, CHOPPED

4 CUPS (960 ML) VEGETABLE BROTH

2 TABLESPOONS LEMON JUICE

I TEASPOON FRESH LEMON THYME LEAVES

¹/3 CUP (75 ML) HEAVY CREAM

FRESHLY GROUND BLACK PEPPER

3 CUPS CHOPPED LEEKS

DICE POTATOES.

In a large pot, melt the butter over medium-high heat. When the foam subsides, add the leeks and garlic. Stir in the salt and cook for 5 minutes, stirring occasion-ally. Add the potatoes and celery. Cook for 10 minutes, stirring frequently to keep the potatoes from sticking. Add the broth and bring to a boil. Reduce the heat and simmer for 20 minutes, or until the potatoes are very tender and easily pierced with a fork. Remove from the heat and stir in the lemon juice and thyme. Puree until completely smooth with an immersion blender or in an upright blender in batches. Stir in the cream and season with pepper. Serve hot.

STIR REGULARLY.

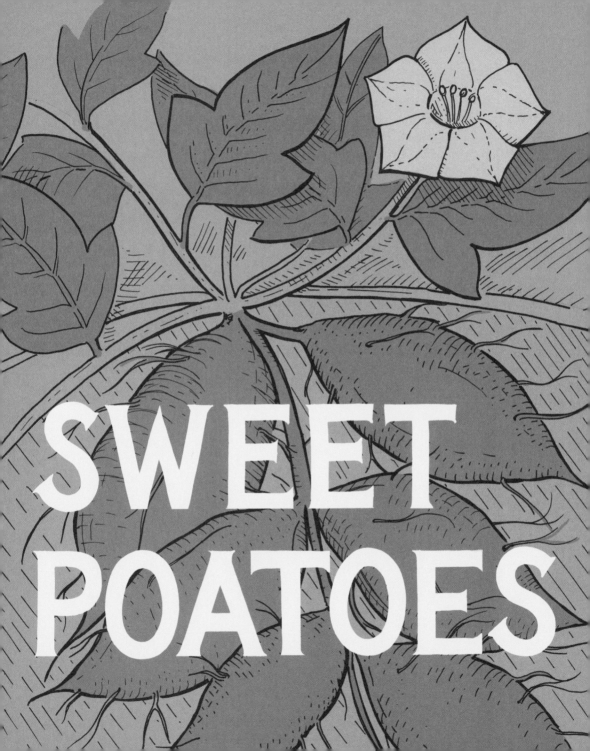

SWEET POATOES

HOW TO GROW SWEET POTATOES

Sweet potatoes are warm-weather plants that do best in hot and sunny climates. In the late summer or fall, the vines yellow, but the potatoes are still growing underground and becoming more nutrient rich. Sweet potatoes can be grown well in large containers or directly in the dirt. They can handle soil that is low in nutrients, but the soil must be loose and well drained for the tubers to grow. Plant slips (root sprouts) about 6 inches (15 cm) deep and 12 inches (30.5 cm) apart with rows spaced about 3 feet (.9 m) apart. The tubers need 90 to 120 days to mature and are harvested after the first frost, so plant with this time frame in mind. About once a week, lift the plant off the ground to prevent it from sending down roots from the vine.

LIFT THE VINE TO KEEP THE PLANT FROM PUTTING DOWN ROOTS.

Once frost has blackened the vine, it's time to harvest them. To harvest, use a shovel to gently loosen the soil 1 to 2 feet (30.5 to 60 cm) around the plant, being careful not to nick any tubers. Use your hands to dig them out of the soil. If you're growing them in a container, simply overturn the container and sift them out. Leave the harvested potatoes in a dry, warm place for 10 days so they sweeten and cure (inside by the heater is a good spot); once cured, store them in a cool and dry place. Cured sweet potatoes will keep for up to 6 months, for use throughout the winter and early spring.

GENTLY LOOSEN DIRT 1 TO 2 FEET AROUND THE PLANT.

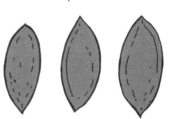

CURE IN A WARM PLACE.

MAKES 12

These savory little hand pies are deeply spiced and have just a touch of natural sweetness from the potatoes. They're great to bring to a potluck, or make them for dinner and have the leftovers for lunch.

FOR THE DOUGH

1 CUP (120 G) WHOLE-WHEAT PASTRY FLOUR

1 CUP (130 G) ALL-PURPOSE FLOUR, OR MORE IF NEEDED

1 TEASPOON SALT

1/3 CUP (75 ML) OLIVE OIL

1/3 TO 1/2 CUP (75 TO 120 ML) WARM WATER

FOR THE FILLING

1 TO 2 TABLESPOONS OLIVE OIL

1 ONION, DICED

2 CLOVES GARLIC, MINCED

2 SWEET POTATOES, PEELED AND CUT INTO
    1/2-INCH (12-MM) CUBES

1 TEASPOON SALT

2 CUPS (370 G) COOKED BLACK BEANS

1/2 TEASPOON FRESHLY GROUND BLACK PEPPER

1 TEASPOON GROUND CUMIN

1/4 TEASPOON GROUND CAYENNE

1/8 TEASPOON GROUND CINNAMON

TO ASSEMBLE

1 EGG

COARSE SALT

Make the dough: In a medium bowl, mix together the flours and salt. Pour in the oil and incorporate with a spoon. Slowly drizzle in the warm water and continue to stir. When you can no longer stir, knead

[CONT.]

it with your fingers. It should be smooth and elastic. If it's overly sticky, add a little more flour. If it seems dry, add a bit more warm water. Cover the bowl with a damp towel or with plastic wrap and let it rest 20 minutes while you prepare the filling.

Make the filling: Heat 1 tablespoon of the oil in a large sauté pan over medium-high heat. Add the onion and garlic and sauté for a minute or two, until they become fragrant. Add the sweet potatoes to the pan and stir in the salt. Cook for 10 minutes, stirring frequently. If the pan becomes dry, add another tablespoon oil. Stir in the beans and cook until they're heated through, about 3 minutes. Remove from the heat and stir in the black pepper, cumin, cayenne, and cinnamon.

MAKE THE FILLING.

Preheat the oven to 450°F (230°C). Line a baking sheet or baking stone with parchment paper, and divide the dough into twelve equal portions. Roll each portion into a small ball, and return them to the bowl; cover with a damp towel while you're working. Roll one portion of dough at a time into a 5- to 6-inch (12- to 15-cm) circle.

Scoop about ¼ cup (60 g) of the sweet potato mixture into the center of one dough round. Fold one side of the

4 TO 6 INCHES

dough over to meet the other side, making a half circle with the filling in the middle. Use a fork to crimp the edges of the dough together and seal the hand pie shut. Transfer the hand pie to the prepared baking sheet. Repeat with the remaining portions. Beat the egg in a bowl and brush the hand pies with the egg wash. Sprinkle with coarse salt. Bake for 20 to 25 minutes, until golden brown. Let cool on a wire rack and serve warm or at room temperature.

BRUSH WITH EGG.

SPRINKLE WITH SALT.

SUBMERGE SLIP IN WATER UNTIL ROOTS FORM.

HOW TO GROW SWEET POTATO SLIPS

Cut an organic sweet potato in half widthwise, and submerge the pieces cut side down in a few inches of water by suspending each in a jar with toothpicks or setting them in a shallow casserole dish. Put the containers on a warm sunny windowsill and monitor them daily, making sure to maintain the water level. In 4 to 6 weeks, your potato will be covered with sprouts. Twist them off from where they emerge from the potato. If the slip already has roots it's ready to be planted; if not, submerge its end in fresh water until roots grow. If it isn't warm enough for them to be transplanted directly, plant them in small pots and keep them indoors until 3 weeks after the expected last frost.

HOW TO GROW LEMONS

Lemons grow best in areas with long growing seasons that don't regularly get below freezing. Plant your tree in an area that receives full sun, isn't too windy, and has soil that drains well. Dwarf varieties, especially Meyer lemons, are successful in large containers (I have a happy little Meyer lemon tree in a container on my back porch). To plant lemons, you can either replant young trees from a nursery or start your own from seed (see page 157). If you're planning to start from seed, select a nice organic lemon from the farmers' market or a friend's tree, remove the seeds, and soak them

PLANT SEEDLINGS WHEN THEY'RE 1-FOOT HIGH.

overnight. In the morning, plant them in a 6-inch (15-cm) pot with moist potting soil. Tie a plastic bag over the top to trap in heat and moisture and set it aside in a warm spot. Check on the pot every few days to make sure the soil hasn't dried out. Once little sprouts emerge (in 2 to 3 weeks), remove the plastic bag and move your seedlings to a sunny window, making sure the soil is moist at all times. When they're about 12 inches (30.5 cm) high, transplant them into your garden or a large container (at least 5 gallons/ 19 L). Lemon trees take about 3 years before they start producing fruit. Once they do, they take a long time to grow

from flower to ripened fruit: 6 to 9 months outdoors, and up to a year inside. Let the lemons ripen completely on the tree, and cut them off with snips when you're ready to use them.

HARVEST RIPE FRUIT USING SNIPS.

FROM FLOWER TO RIPE FRUIT MAY TAKE UP TO 1 YEAR.

SERVES 6

These individual little cakes pack a surprise: As they bake, the cake separates into two layers! The top is a tender, moist sponge cake, while the bottom becomes a delicious citrus custard. They're warm, tart, and delicious on any chilly evening, either on their own or served with a small scoop of vanilla ice cream.

³/4 CUP (150 G) GRANULATED SUGAR

4 TABLESPOONS (55 G) UNSALTED BUTTER, AT ROOM TEMPERATURE

3 EGGS, SEPARATED

I TABLESPOON FINELY GRATED LEMON ZEST (FROM ABOUT 2 LEMONS)

I TEASPOON VANILLA EXTRACT

¹/3 CUP (40 G) ALL-PURPOSE FLOUR

¹/4 TEASPOON SALT

³/4 CUP (180 ML) WHOLE MILK

6 TABLESPOONS (90 ML) LEMON JUICE
(FROM ABOUT 3 LEMONS)

I TABLESPOON CONFECTIONERS' SUGAR

Preheat the oven to 350°F (175°C). In a large bowl, cream together the granulated sugar and 3 tablespoons of the butter with an electric mixer on medium-high speed until well blended. Beat in the egg yolks one at a time, until well incorporated. Mix in the lemon zest and vanilla. Add the flour and salt and stir with a rubber spatula until combined. Gradually stir in the milk and lemon juice.

Set the batter aside and, in a separate bowl with an electric mixer and clean beaters, whip the egg whites on high speed until stiff peaks form. Fold the egg whites into the batter in three additions

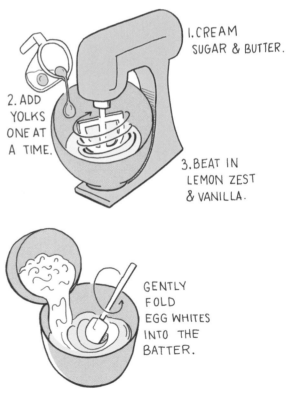

1. CREAM SUGAR & BUTTER.

2. ADD YOLKS ONE AT A TIME.

3. BEAT IN LEMON ZEST & VANILLA.

GENTLY FOLD EGG WHITES INTO THE BATTER.

[CONT.]

until just incorporated. Grease six 4-ounce (118-ml) ramekins with the remaining 1 tablespoon butter. Divide the batter evenly among the ramekins. Set the ramekins in a 9-by-13-inch (23-by-33-cm) baking dish (or any size that will accommodate them), then carefully pour hot water into the baking dish so that it comes about halfway up the sides of the ramekins. Carefully transfer the baking dish to the oven and bake for 40 to 45 minutes, until golden brown. Remove from the oven, then transfer the ramekins from the water bath to a towel on the counter. Let cool for 10 to 15 minutes and dust with the confectioners' sugar before serving.

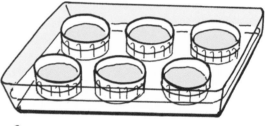

BAKE IN A HOT WATER BATH.

HOW TO START A LEMON TREE

1. PICK THE SEEDS OUT OF A LEMON.

2. SOAK OVERNIGHT.

3. PLANT THE SEEDS IN A POT. WATER. TIE A PLASTIC BAG OVER TOP TO TRAP HEAT & MOISTURE.

6 IN. (15 CM)

4. DON'T LET THE SOIL DRY OUT. SPROUTS WILL EMERGE IN 2 TO 3 WEEKS.

5. ONCE SPROUTS EMERGE, REMOVE THE BAG & THIN TO 1 SPROUT PER POT.

6. TRANSPLANT WHEN THE TREE IS 12 IN. (30 CM) TALL.

Although we can get carried away with the bounty of the spring and summer harvest, there's a thin line between having an abundance of produce and having your bumper crop end up in the compost. This section includes a few different methods for stowing away your produce for cooler days, so you can enjoy the freshness of your garden as the growing season slows. Drying herbs, canning, and making your own pickles may seem quaint, but it's decidedly practical if you're going to be growing your own food.

ESSENTIAL TOOLS FOR PRESERVING

JARS

NEW LIDS

RINGS

CANNER POT

SAUCE POT:
FOR SANITIZING
LIDS & RINGS

JAR LIFTER

TONGS

BUTTER KNIFE
OR OTHER LONG
IMPLEMENT

CLEAN KITCHEN TOWELS

PRESERVING YOUR HERBS

HOW TO DRY HERBS

Using the herbs from your garden in a recipe is incredibly satisfying, but you often end up with more than you can use during a growing season. Herbs that are low in moisture, such as sage, thyme, dill, bay leaves, rosemary, and marjoram, take to drying well. Make sure to harvest your herbs at peak flavor and discard any blemished leaves and stems before you get started.

1. Lightly mist or rinse herbs to remove soil and pat dry.

2. Bundle 4 to 6 branches or sprigs and hang them upside down in a shady and well-ventilated spot.

3. Check every 2 days. When the leaves easily crumble, they are dry.

4. Store your herbs whole in airtight containers in a cool, dry place. Crush them right before use. They will keep for a year.

PESTO SAUCE
MAKES I CUP (240 ML)

Pesto sauce is my favorite way to use up my stores of basil, cilantro, mint, or parsley and it's incredibly versatile. Traditionally, it's made with a mortar and pestle, but it comes together quickly and easily in a food processor.

---

2 CUPS (80 G) FRESH HERBS (SEE NOTE)

1/2 CUP (120 ML) OLIVE OIL, OR MORE IF NEEDED

2 TABLESPOONS PINE NUTS OR WALNUTS, LIGHTLY TOASTED

I CLOVE GARLIC

PINCH OF SALT

Combine the herbs, half of the oil, the pine nuts, garlic, and salt in a food processor. Pulse for a few seconds. Scrape down the sides and repeat, gradually adding the rest of the oil until you've reached your desired consistency. Fresh pesto keeps for a week in the refrigerator or months in the freezer. If freezing, pour a layer of oil over the top once it's in the container to protect the delicate leaves from frostbite. Be sure to leave some headspace in your jar for the pesto to expand as it freezes.

NOTE:

Basil is typically used for pesto, but I like cilantro, mint, and parsley, too. If using basil, I often mix in ½ cup (60 g) grated Parmesan cheese right before serving.

2 CUPS OF HERBS

1/2 CUP OLIVE OIL

- 2 CUPS HERBS
- 1/4 CUP+ OLIVE OIL
- 2 TABLESPOONS
- PINE NUTS
- I CLOVE GARLIC
- PINCH OF SALT

PRESERVING VEGETABLES AND FRUITS

While drying works great for preserving herbs, vegetables and fruits respond best to canning and pickling. Here are my favorite ways to continue enjoying my bounty well into the off-season.

HOME CANNING

The most important rule of canning is to keep everything clean: Before you get started, wash your jars, lids, utensils, your hands, and the countertop, and always use clean towels. Jars and jar rings can be reused from season to season, but lids must be new to create a proper seal. It's also important to use only the freshest, blemish-free produce—you don't want to introduce bacteria into the food. The process described here is called "boiling water bath canning," and it works with heat and acidity to prevent bacteria growth and spoilage. This process only works with high-acid fruits and pickles. If you want to preserve vegetables that are low in acid, such as carrots, you have to either add vinegar (acid) to make them into pickles (as on page 169) or use a high-pressure canning method involving a pressure canner, which we won't be discussing here.

CANNING BASICS

1. Prepare your produce according to the recipe you're following.

2. Sterilize all jars, rings, and any utensils you'll be using in a large pot of boiling water for 10 minutes. If your canning pot doesn't have a grate at the bottom, place a white dishtowel in the bottom of the pot of water to help protect the jars from cracking. When done, turn off the heat, but leave the jars in the water until you're ready to pack them.

BOIL JARS FOR 5 MIN.

PLACE GRATE OR TOWEL IN THE BOTTOM.

PLACE LIDS, RINGS & OTHER IMPLEMENTS IN BOILING WATER. TURN OFF HEAT.

3. Bring a small pot of water to a boil, remove from heat, and drop the lids in. Leave them in the water until you're ready to seal your jars.

4. Remove the jars from the water with a jar lifter and set them upright on a dry kitchen towel on the counter. Pack them with whatever it is you're canning, filling the jar almost to the top, but leaving ¼ to ½ inch (6 to 12 mm) of headspace. Run a clean butter knife around the inside edge of the jar to remove any air pockets.

5. Use the tongs to fish out a lid, wipe the rim of the jar clean with a clean damp cloth, and place the lid on the jar and secure it with a ring, screwing it on finger tight—that is, firmly but not too tight. Repeat with the rest of the jars.

6. Lower the jars right side up into your canner pot filled with hot water (you can use the same water you used to sterilize your jars). The water should cover the jars by at least 1 inch (2.5 cm). Bring the water to a full boil and process according to the recipe you're following.

RUN THE BUTTER KNIFE AROUND THE EDGE OF THE JAR.

WIPE THE EDGE CLEAN.

⌐LEAVE ¼ TO ½ IN. HEADSPACE.

↙AIR POCKETS (THESE ARE BAD.)

PLACE NEW LID ON JAR & SCREW ON RING.

⌐ JARS SHOULD BE COVERED BY AT LEAST 1 IN. OF WATER.

BRING TO A BOIL.

7. Use the jar lifter to remove the jars from the water and set them on a dry towel to cool. As the jars cool, you will hear a distinct "pop" when the jar seals, and center of the lid is sucked in. Test to make sure the lids have sealed by pushing down on the center. If a lid has sealed properly, it shouldn't have any give. If any jars don't seal, put them in the refrigerator and use first. Sealed jars will keep for at least 1 year.

POP!

LIDS ARE
SUCKED
IN.

PUSH ON
THE CENTER
OF THE LID.
THERE SHOULD
BE NO GIVE.

CANNED TOMATOES
MAKES 4 1-PINT (480-ML) JARS

Home–canned tomatoes are much better than any you can buy at the store. This is because you're assured that the tomatoes you preserve were vine ripened and canned at peak freshness. Some tomatoes are acidic enough to can safely, but it's safer to add lemon juice to each jar.

---

5 POUNDS (2.3 KG) RIPE TOMATOES CORED, PEELED, HALVED, AND SEEDED (SEE PAGE 68), JUICE RESERVED

4 TABLESPOONS (60 ML) LEMON JUICE

Sterilize 4 1-pint (480-ml) jars as described on page 164; gather clean rings and new lids. Pack the tomato halves into the hot jars tightly, leaving ¼ to ½ inch (6 to 12 mm) of headspace. Add 1 tablespoon lemon juice to each pint jar of tomatoes. Strain the seeds from the reserved juice and pour it level with the tomato halves, being sure to leave headspace. Sweep a butter knife around the inside of each jar to remove air bubbles. Wipe the rims of the jars and screw on the lids. Place the jars in the canner pot and make sure the water covers the jars by at least 1 inch (2.5 cm). Boil for 1 hour 15 minutes. Remove the jars from the water with a jar lifter, then let them cool on a kitchen towel. Refrigerate any jars that haven't sealed.

PACK THEM DOWN.

1 TBS. LEMON JUICE IN EACH JAR

FILL JAR, LEAVING ¼ TO ½ IN. HEADSPACE.

WIPE RIM CLEAN & SCREW ON LID.

POUR STRAINED TOMATO JUICE LEVEL WITH THE TOMATO HALVES.

PROCESS FOR 85 MIN.

RASPBERRY JAM

MAKES 6 HALF-PINT (240 ML) JARS

In the spring and summer, berries are bountiful but often for only a brief window. Making jam or preserves keeps them around longer, to be swirled into yogurt or spread on toast.

4 CUPS RASPBERRIES

---

4 CUPS (672 G) RASPBERRIES

4 CUPS (800 G) GRANULATED SUGAR

I TABLESPOON LEMON JUICE

Sterilize 6 half-pint (240 ml) jars according to the instructions on page 164. Put the raspberries in a large pot, mash them with a potato masher or the back of a spoon, and bring to a boil over medium heat. Boil for 2 minutes. Add the sugar and lemon juice to the raspberries and stir to dissolve the sugar. Return the mixture to a boil and cook for 4 minutes. Pour the jam into hot sterilized jars, wipe the rims of the jars clean, and screw on the lids. Let them cool on the countertop. There is enough sugar and acid in the fruit that further processing in a boiling water bath is unnecessary. As always, refrigerate any jars of jam that don't seal.

4 CUPS SUGAR

1 TBS. LEMON JUICE

YOUR HOMEMADE JAM!

LEMON JUICE

PICKLING

While low-acid vegetables can be made into pickles and canned to be shelf stable, refrigerator pickles are my favorite quick and easy way to extend my harvest. These don't have a long shelf life like canned pickles, but they maintain their crunchy texture and they're easy to make in small batches. Because they're chilled, the process doesn't require the same amount of diligence to prevent spoilage and other nasties like botulism.

REFRIGERATOR PICKLES
MAKES I QUART (960 ML) JAR

Refrigerator pickles can be made out of any firm vegetables that can be eaten raw. Carrots, zucchini, peppers, onions, and cucumbers are all good options. Smaller vegetables like green beans can be pickled whole, but larger veggies like cucumbers should be cut lengthwise into ½- to ¾-inch (12- to 19-mm) pieces to make long skinny spears.

---

³/4 TO I POUND (340 TO 455 G) BLEMISH-FREE VEGETABLES OF YOUR CHOICE, CLEANED AND CUT

I ¼ CUPS (300 ML) APPLE CIDER VINEGAR (SEE NOTE, PAGE 170)

¼ CUP (50 G) GRANULATED SUGAR

2 TABLESPOONS SALT

I TABLESPOON MUSTARD SEEDS

I TEASPOON WHOLE BLACK PEPPERCORNS

I BAY LEAF

Tightly pack a clean quart (960 ml) jar with your vegetables. Make the brine: In a saucepan, combine the vinegar, ¾ cup (180 ml) water, the sugar, salt, mustard seeds, peppercorns, and bay leaf. Bring to a boil and stir to dissolve the sugar and salt. Boil for 2 minutes. Pour the hot brine into the jar with the vegetables, leaving ½ inch (12 mm) of headspace. Screw on the lid and shake gently

[CONT.]

to distribute the spices. Let the pickles cool on the countertop, then refrigerate and let the flavors meld for about a week before eating. The pickles will keep in the refrigerator for 2 months.

NOTE:

Distilled white vinegar can also be used, but is less flavorful.

HOT BRINE

3/4 POUND VEGGIES

BRINE:
- 1 1/4 CUP APPLE CIDER VINEGAR
- 3/4 CUP WATER
- 1/4 SUGAR
- 2 TBS. SALT
- 1 TBS. MUSTARD SEEDS
- 1 TSP. PEPPERCORN
- 1 BAY LEAF

ACKNOWLEDGMENTS

First and foremost, I would like to thank Cristina Garces, my editor. Her input and guidance from the very beginning have been invaluable. This book is as much hers as it is mine, and without her unwavering support and encouragement this project would have seemed impossible. Big thanks to everyone else at Stewart, Tabori & Chang for giving me the opportunity to make this book. To Andrew Myers, my sweet boyfriend, for all his love, patience, and for making me dinner when I was too busy writing and drawing about cooking to actually do it. Thank you to Damon Styer of New Bohemia Signs, and the entire NBS crew, for teaching me everything I know about lettering and sign painting, and for their continued support and friendship. Thanks also to all my studio mates at the Compound, for all their input, and critical feedback. Thanks to James T. Edmondson, for making a font out of my painted letters for the headers of this book. Thanks to all my friends and family who helped test recipes. To my sister Tina, for all her loving help with my graphic design questions. And of course, thank you to my parents, grandmother, and sister Sarah for their unwavering love and support.

Finally, thank you to everyone who is part of the San Francisco Bay Area food culture. From Alice Waters, to my neighbor who grows artichokes next to her mailbox, the vibrance and variety of growers, cooks, and DIY makers is what makes the Bay special and a hugely inspirational place to live, and that inspiration is the soul of this book.

SOURCES

GARDENING AND COOKING BOOKS

Barrington, Vanessa. *D.I.Y. Delicious: Recipes and Ideas for Simple Food from Scratch.* San Francisco: Chronicle Books, 2010.

Bittman, Mark. *How to Cook Everything.* Hoboken, NJ: John Wiley & Sons, Inc., 1998.

Chesman, Andrea. *The Pickled Pantry.* North Adams, MA: Storey, 2012.

Coyne, Kelly, and Erik Knutzen. *The Urban Homestead: Your Guide to Self-Sufficient Living in the Heart of the City.* Port Townsend, WA: Process Media, 2010.

Creasy, Rosalind. *Edible Landscaping.* San Francisco: Sierra Club Books, 2010.

Fowler, Alys. *Garden Anywhere: How to Grow Gorgeous Container Gardens, Herb Gardens, Kitchen Gardens, and More, Without Spending a Fortune.* San Francisco: Chronicle Books, 2009.

Hirsheimer, Christopher, and Peggy Knickerbocker. *The San Francisco Ferry Plaza Farmers' Market Cookbook: A Comprehensive Guide to Impeccable Produce Plus 130 Seasonal Recipes.* San Francisco: Chronicle Books, 2006.

Peirce, Pam. *Golden Gate Gardening: The Complete Guide to Year-Round Food Gardening in the San Francisco Bay Area and Coastal California.* Seattle: Sasquatch Books, 2010.

The Edible Garden. Menlo Park, CA: Sunset Books, 2005.

Waters, Alice, and Kelsie Kerr. *The Art of Simple Food II.* New York: Clarkson Potter, 2013.

HELPFUL GARDENING WEBSITES

www.almanac.com
www.bonnieplants.com
www.motherearthnews.com/organic-gardening
www.organicgardening.com

RESOURCES

CANNING SUPPLIES:
Ball
www.freshpreserving.com

CHOCOLATE:
Tcho Chocolate
www.tcho.com

FLOURS AND WHOLE GRAINS:
Bob's Red Mill
www.bobsredmill.com

KITCHEN EQUIPMENT:
Sur la Table
www.surlatable.com

MAPLE SYRUP:
Vermont Maple Sugar Makers Association
www.vermontmaple.org

OLIVE OIL:
California Olive Oil Council
www.cooc.com

SEEDS & GARDEN SUPPLY:
Baker Creek Heirloom Seeds
www.rareseeds.com

Johnny's Selected Seeds
www.johnnyseeds.com

Peaceful Valley Farm & Garden Supply
www.groworganic.com

Seeds Savers Exchange
www.seedsavers.org

INDEX